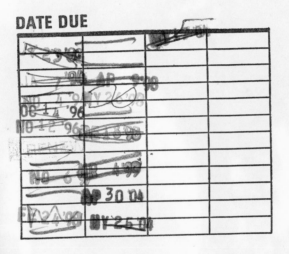

Modern Critical Interpretations

Charles Dickens's
A Tale of Two Cities

Modern Critical Interpretations

These and other titles in preparation

Charles Dickens's
A Tale of Two Cities

Edited and with an introduction by
Harold Bloom
Sterling Professor of the Humanities
Yale University

Chelsea House Publishers ◊ *1987*
NEW YORK ◊ NEW HAVEN ◊ PHILADELPHIA

© 1987 by Chelsea House Publishers,
a division of Chelsea House Educational Communications, Inc.,
  95 Madison Avenue, New York, NY 10016
  345 Whitney Avenue, New Haven, CT 06511
  5014 West Chester Pike, Edgemont, PA 19028

Introduction © 1987 by Harold Bloom

Printed and bound in the United States of America

10 9 8 7 6 5 4 3 2 1

∞ The paper used in this publication meets the minimum
requirements of the American National Standard for Permanence
of Paper for Printed Library Materials, Z39.48–1984.

Library of Congress Cataloging-in-Publication Data
Charles Dickens's A tale of two cities.
  (Modern critical interpretations)
  Bibliography: p.
  Includes index.
  1. Dickens, Charles, 1812–1870.   Tale of two cities.
2. France—History—Revolution, 1789–1799—Literature and
the revolution.   I. Bloom, Harold.   II. Series.
PR4571.C48   1987   823'.8   87–9355
ISBN 0–87754–738–6 (alk. paper)

Contents

Editor's Note

This book gathers together a representative selection of the best modern criticism devoted to Charles Dickens's novel *A Tale of Two Cities*. The critical essays are reprinted here in the chronological order of their original publication. I am grateful to Neil Arditi for his labor as a researcher for this volume.

My introduction, after suggesting Ruskin's "stage fire" as a critical trope for the understanding of Dickens, discusses Madame Defarge as a nightmare image of Dickens's desire. Robert Alter begins the chronological sequence with a historical view of daemonic elements in the *Tale*. In the essay of David D. Marcus, we receive a new perspective concerning Carlyle's influence on Dickens's novel.

Albert D. Hutter explores themes of fatherhood and parricide in the *Tale*, while John Kucich carries the same dark enquiry forward into the book's veritable festival of released violence.

Catherine Gallagher's study of doubling and duplicity considers revolution, resurrection, and execution as violent tropes for writing in the *Tale*. Charles Darnay, rarely defended by modern critics, receives respectful consideration from Edwin M. Eigner.

Drowning in truth and in metaphor is the emphasis in Garrett Stewart's exegesis of the *Tale*. With J. M. Rignall's study of catastrophe through continuity, we come back full circle to Alter's view of the demons of history in Dickens's revolutionary nightmare, and so also end where we began in my introduction, with Madame Defarge, at once attractive and sinister, and yet the Muse of *A Tale of Two Cities*.

Introduction

Courage would be the critical virtue most required if anyone were to attempt an essay that might be called "The Limitations of Shakespeare." Tolstoy, in his most outrageous critical performance, more or less tried just that, with dismal results, and even Ben Jonson might not have done much better, had he sought to extend his ambivalent *obiter dicta* on his great friend and rival. Nearly as much courage, or foolhardiness, is involved in discoursing on the limitations of Dickens, but the young Henry James had a critical gusto that could carry him through every literary challenge. Reviewing *Our Mutual Friend* in 1865, James exuberantly proclaimed that "*Bleak House* was forced; *Little Dorrit* was labored; the present work is dug out as with a spade and pickaxe." At about this time, reviewing *Drum-Taps,* James memorably dismissed Whitman as an essentially prosaic mind seeking to lift itself, by muscular exertion, into poetry. To reject some of the major works of the strongest English novelist and the greatest American poet, at about the same moment, is to set standards for critical audacity that no one since has been able to match, even as no novelist since has equalled Dickens, nor any poet, Walt Whitman.

James was at his rare worst in summing up Dickens's supposedly principal inadequacy:

> Such scenes as this are useful in fixing the limits of Mr. Dickens's insight. Insight is, perhaps, too strong a word; for we are convinced that it is one of the chief conditions of his genius not to see beneath the surface of things. If we might hazard a definition of his literary character, we should, accordingly, call him the greatest of superficial novelists. We are aware that this definition confines him to an inferior

rank in the department of letters which he adorns; but we
accept this consequence of our proposition. It were, in our
opinion, an offence against humanity to place Mr. Dickens
among the greatest novelists. For, to repeat what we have
already intimated, he has created nothing but figure. He has
added nothing to our understanding of human character. He
is master of but two alternatives: he reconciles us to what is
commonplace, and he reconciles us to what is odd. The
value of the former service is questionable; and the manner
in which Mr. Dickens performs it sometimes conveys a
certain impression of charlatanism. The value of the latter
service is incontestable, and here Mr. Dickens is an honest,
an admirable artist.

This can be taken literally, and then transvalued: to see truly the
surface of things, to reconcile us at once to the commonplace and the
odd—these are not minor gifts. In 1860, John Ruskin, the great seer of
the surface of things, the charismatic illuminator of the commonplace
and the odd together, had reached a rather different conclusion from
that of the young Henry James, five years before James's brash rejection:

> The essential value and truth of Dickens's writings have
> been unwisely lost sight of by many thoughtful persons
> merely because he presents his truth with some colour of
> caricature. Unwisely, because Dickens's caricature, though
> often gross, is never mistaken. Allowing for his manner of
> telling them, the things he tells us are always true. I wish
> that he could think it right to limit his brilliant exaggeration
> to works written only for public amusement; and when he
> takes up a subject of high national importance, such as that
> which he handled in *Hard Times,* that he would use severer
> and more accurate analysis. The usefulness of that work (to
> my mind, in several respects, the greatest he has written) is
> with many persons seriously diminished because Mr. Bound-
> erby is a dramatic monster, instead of a characteristic exam-
> ple of a worldly master; and Stephen Blackpool a dramatic
> perfection, instead of a characteristic example of an honest
> workman. But let us not lose the use of Dickens's wit and
> insight, because he chooses to speak in a circle of stage fire.
> He is entirely right in his main drift and purpose in every
> book he has written; and all of them, but especially *Hard*

Times, should be studied with close and earnest care by persons interested in social questions. They will find much that is partial, and, because partial, apparently unjust; but if they examine all the evidence on the other side, which Dickens seems to overlook, it will appear, after all their trouble, that his view was the finally right one, grossly and sharply told.

To say of Dickens that he chose "to speak in a circle of stage fire" is exactly right, since Dickens is the greatest actor among novelists, the finest master of dramatic projection. A superb stage performer, he never stops performing in his novels, which is not the least of his many Shakespearean characteristics. Martin Price usefully defines some of these as "his effortless invention, his brilliant play of language, the scope and density of his imagined world." I like also Price's general comparison of Dickens to the strongest satirist in the language, Swift, a comparison that Price shrewdly turns into a confrontation:

> But the confrontation helps us to define differences as well: Dickens is more explicit, more overtly compassionate, insisting always upon the perversions of feeling as well as of thought. His outrage is of the same consistency as his generous celebration, the satirical wit of the same copious extravagance as the comic elaborations. Dickens' world is alive with things that snatch, lurch, teeter, thrust, leer; it is the animate world of Netherlandish genre painting or of Hogarth's prints, where all space is a field of force, where objects vie or intrigue with each other, where every human event spills over into the things that surround it. This may become the typically crowded scene of satire, where persons are reduced to things and things to matter in motion; or it may pulsate with fierce energy and noisy feeling. It is different from Swift; it is the distinctive Dickensian plenitude, which we find again in his verbal play, in his great array of vivid characters, in his massed scenes of feasts or public declamations. It creates rituals as compelling as the resuscitation of Rogue Riderhood, where strangers participate solemnly in the recovery of a spark of life, oblivious for the moment of the unlovely human form it will soon inhabit.

That animate, Hogarthian world, "where all space is a field of force," indeed is a plenitude and it strikes me that Price's vivid description suggests Rabelais rather than Swift as a true analogue. Dickens, like Shakespeare in one of many aspects and like Rabelais, is as much carnival as stage fire, a kind of endless festival. The reader of Dickens stands in the midst of a festival, which is too varied, too multiform, to be taken in even by innumerable readings. Something always escapes our ken; Ben Jonson's sense of being "rammed with life" is exemplified more even by Dickens than by Rabelais, in that near-Shakespearean plenitude that is Dickens's peculiar glory.

Is it possible to define that plenitude narrowly enough so as to conceptualize it for critical use, though by "conceptualize" one meant only a critical metaphor? Shakespearean representation is no touchstone for Dickens or for anyone else, since above all modes of representation it turns upon an inward changing brought about by characters listening to themselves speak. Dickens cannot do that. His villains are gorgeous, but there are no Iagos or Edmunds among them. The severer, more relevant test, which Dickens must fail, though hardly to his detriment, is Falstaff, who generates not only his own meaning, but meaning in so many others besides, both on and off the page. Probably the severest test is Shylock, most Dickensian of Shakespeare's characters, since we cannot say of Dickens's Shylock, Fagin, that there is much Shakespearean about him at all. Fagin is a wonderful grotesque, but the winds of will are not stirred in him, while they burn on hellishly forever in Shylock.

Carlyle's injunction, to work in the will, seems to have little enough place in the cosmos of the Dickens characters. I do not say this to indicate a limitation, or even a limit, nor do I believe that the will to live or the will to power is ever relaxed in or by Dickens. But nothing is got for nothing, except perhaps in or by Shakespeare, and Dickens purchases his kind of plenitude at the expense of one aspect of the will. T. S. Eliot remarked that "Dickens's characters are real because there is no one like them." I would modify that to "They are real because they are not like one another, though sometimes they are a touch more like some of us than like each other." Perhaps the will, in whatever aspect, can differ only in degree rather than in kind among us. The aesthetic secret of Dickens appears to be that his villains, heroes, heroines, victims, eccentrics, ornamental beings, do differ from one another *in the kinds of will that they possess*. Since that is hardly possible for us, as humans, it does bring about an absence in reality in and for Dickens. That is a high price to pay, but it is a good deal less than everything and Dickens got more than he paid for. We also receive a great deal more than we ever are asked to surrender when we read Dickens. That may indeed be his most Shakespearean quality, and may provide the critical trope I quest for in him. James and Proust hurt you more than Dickens does, and the hurt is the meaning, or much of it. What hurts in Dickens never has much to do with meaning, because there cannot be a poetics of pain where the will has ceased to be common or sadly uniform. Dickens really does offer a poetics of pleasure, which is surely worth our secondary uneasiness at his refusal to offer us any accurately mimetic representations of the human will. He writes always the book of the drives, which is why supposedly Freudian readings of him always fail so tediously. The conceptual metaphor he suggests in his representations of character and personality is neither Shakespearean mirror nor Romantic lamp, neither Rabelaisian carnival nor Fieldingesque open country. "Stage fire" seems to me perfect, for "stage" removes something of the reality of the will, yet only as modifier. The substantive remains "fire." Dickens is the poet of the fire of the drives, the true celebrant of Freud's myth of frontier concepts, of that domain lying on the border between psyche and body, falling into matter, yet partaking of the reality of both.

II

Except perhaps for *Pickwick Papers, A Tale of Two Cities* always has been the most popular of Dickens's books, if we set aside also the annual phenomenon of *A Christmas Carol* and the other Christmas books. No critic however would rank it with such other later novels as *Great Expectations* and *Our Mutual Friend* or the unfinished *Edwin Drood,* or with the many earlier and middle period masterpieces. The harshest single judgment remains that of the now forgotten but formidably pungent reviewer Sir James Fitzjames Stephen, who left Dickens nothing:

> The moral tone of the *Tale of Two Cities* is not more wholesome than that of its predecessors, nor does it display any nearer approach to a solid knowledge of the subject-matter to which it refers. Mr. Dickens observes in his preface—"It has been one of my hopes to add something to the popular and picturesque means of understanding that terrible time, though no one can hope to add anything to the philosophy

of Mr. Carlyle's wonderful book." The allusion to Mr.
Carlyle confirms the presumption which the book itself
raises, that Mr. Dickens happened to have read the *History
of the French Revolution,* and, being on the look-out for a
subject, determined off-hand to write a novel about it.
Whether he has any other knowledge of the subject than a
single reading of Mr. Carlyle's work would supply does not
appear, but certainly what he has written shows no more. It
is exactly the sort of story which a man would write who
had taken down Mr. Carlyle's theory without any sort of
inquiry or examination, but with a comfortable conviction
that "nothing could be added to its philosophy." The people, says Mr. Dickens, in effect, had been degraded by long
and gross misgovernment, and acted like wild beasts in consequence. There is, no doubt, a great deal of truth in this
view of the matter, but it is such very elementary truth that,
unless a man had something new to say about it, it is hardly
worth mentioning; and Mr. Dickens supports it by specific
assertions which, if not absolutely false, are at any rate so
selected as to convey an entirely false impression. It is a
shameful thing for a popular writer to exaggerate the faults
of the French aristocracy in a book which will naturally find
its way to readers who know very little of the subject except
what he chooses to tell them; but it is impossible not to feel
that the melodramatic story which Mr. Dickens tells about
the wicked Marquis who violates one of his serfs and murders another, is a grossly unfair representation of the state of
society in France in the middle of the eighteenth century.
That the French *noblesse* had much to answer for in a thousand ways, is a lamentable truth; but it is by no means true
that they could rob, murder, and ravish with impunity.
When Count Horn thought proper to try the experiment
under the Regency, he was broken on the wheel, notwith-
standing his nobility; and the sort of atrocities which Mr.
Dickens depicts as characteristic of the eighteenth century
were neither safe nor common in the fourteenth.

The most palpable hit here is certainly Dickens's extraordinary
reliance upon Carlyle's bizarre but effective *French Revolution,* which is
not the history it purports to be but rather has the design, rhetoric, and

vision of an apocalyptic fantasy. No one now would read either Carlyle or Dickens in order to learn anything about the French Revolution, and sadly enough no one now reads Carlyle anyway. Yet Stephen's dismay remains legitimate; countless thousands continue to receive the only impressions they ever will have of the French Revolution through the reading of *A Tale of Two Cities*. The book remains a great tale, a vivid instance of Dickens's preternatural gifts as a pure storyteller, though except for its depiction of the superbly ghastly Madame Defarge and her Jacobin associates it lacks the memorable grotesques and driven enthusiasts that we expect from Dickens.

The most palpable flaw in the novel is the weakness as representations of Lucie and Darnay, and the relative failure of the more crucial Carton, who simply lacks the aesthetic dignity that Dickens so desperately needed to give him. If Carton and Darnay, between them, really were meant to depict the spiritual form of Charles Dickens, then their mutual lack of gusto renders them even more inadequate. When Madame Defarge dies, slain by her own bullet, we are very moved, particularly by relief that such an unrelenting version of the death drive will cease to menace us. When Carton, looking "sublime and prophetic," goes to execution, Dickens attempts to move us: we receive the famous and unacceptable, "It is a far, far better thing that I do, than I have ever done; it is a far, far better rest that I go to than I have ever known." Dickens owes us a far, far better rhetoric than that, and generally he delivers it.

The life of *A Tale of Two Cities* is elsewhere, centered upon the negative sublimity of Madame Defarge and her knitting, which is one of Dickens's finest inventions, and is clearly a metaphor for the storytelling of the novel itself. Dickens hardly would have said: "I am Madame Defarge," but she, like the author, remorselessly controls the narrative, until she loses her struggle with the epitome of a loving Englishwoman, Miss Pross. The book's penultimate chapter, in which we are rid of Madame Defarge, is shrewdly called "The Knitting Done."

Even Dickens rarely surpasses the nightmare intensity of Madame Defarge, her absolute command of stage fire, and his finest accomplishment in the book is to increase her already stark aura as the narrative knits onwards. Here is a superb early epiphany of the lady, putting heart into her formidable husband, who seems weak only in comparison to his wife, less a force of nature than of history:

The night was hot, and the shop, close shut and surrounded by so foul a neighbourhood, was ill-smelling. Monsieur Defarge's olfactory sense was by no means delicate, but the stock of wine smelt much stronger than it ever tasted, and so did the stock of rum and brandy and aniseed. He whiffed the compound of scents away, as he put down his smoked-out pipe.

"You are fatigued," said madame, raising her glance as she knotted the money. "There are only the usual odours."

"I am a little tired," her husband acknowledged.

"You are a little depressed, too," said madame, whose quick eyes had never been so intent on the accounts, but they had had a ray or two for him. "Oh, the men, the men!"

"But my dear!" began Defarge.

"But my dear!" repeated madame, nodding firmly; "but my dear! You are faint of heart to-night, my dear!"

"Well, then," said Defarge, as if a thought were wrung out of his breast, "it *is* a long time."

"It is a long time," repeated his wife; "and when is it not a long time? Vengeance and retribution require a long time; it is the rule."

"It does not take a long time to strike a man with Lightning," said Defarge.

"How long," demanded madame, composely, "does it take to make and store the lightning? Tell me."

Defarge raised his head thoughtfully, as if there were something in that too.

"It does not take a long time," said madame, "for an earthquake to swallow a town. Eh well! Tell me how long it takes to prepare the earthquake?"

"A long time, I suppose," said Defarge.

"But when it is ready, it takes place, and grinds to pieces everything before it. In the meantime, it is always preparing, though it is not seen or heard. That is your consolation. Keep it."

She tied a knot with flashing eyes, as if it throttled a foe.

"I tell thee," said madame, extending her right hand, for emphasis, "that although it is a long time on the road, it is on the road and coming. I tell thee it never retreats, and never stops. I tell thee it is always advancing. Look around and consider the lives of all the world that we know, consider the faces of all the world that we know, consider the rage and discontent to which the Jacquerie addresses itself with more and more of certainty every hour. Can such things last? Bah! I mock you."

"My brave wife," returned Defarge, standing before her with his head a little bent, and his hands clasped at his back, like a docile and attentive pupil before his catechist, "I do not question all this. But it has lasted a long time, and it is possible—you know well, my wife, it is possible—that it may not come, during our lives."

"Eh well! How then?" demanded madame, tying another knot, as if there were another enemy strangled.

"Well!" said Defarge, with a half-complaining and half-apologetic shrug. "We shall not see the triumph."

"We shall have helped it," returned madame, with her extended hand in strong action. "Nothing that we do, is done in vain. I believe, with all my soul, that we shall see the triumph. But even if not, even if I knew certainly not, show me the neck of an aristocrat and tyrant, and still I would—"

Then madame, with her teeth set, tied a very terrible knot indeed.

"Hold!" cried Defarge, reddening a little as if he felt charged with cowardice; "I too, my dear, will stop at nothing."

"Yes! But it is your weakness that you sometimes need to see your victim and your opportunity, to sustain you. Sustain yourself without that. When the time comes, let loose a tiger and a devil; but wait for the time with the tiger and the devil chained—not shown—yet always ready."

To be always preparing, unseen and unheard, is Madame Defarge's one consolation. Dickens has made her childless, somewhat in the mysterious mode of Lady Macbeth, since somehow we believe that Madame Defarge too must have nursed an infant. Her dialogue with Defarge has overtones of Lady Macbeth heartening Macbeth, keying up his resolution to treason and a kind of parricide. What Dickens has learned from Shakespeare is the art of counterpointing degrees of terror, of excess, so as to suggest a dread that otherwise would reside beyond representation. Macbeth, early doubting, seems weak in contrast to his wife's force, but we will see him at his bloody work, until he becomes an astonishing manifestation of tyranny. Similarly, Defarge seems little in juxtaposition to his implacable wife, but we will see him as a demon of courage, skill, and apocalyptic drive, leading the triumphant assault upon the Bastille.

In his final vision of Madame Defarge, Dickens brilliantly reveals his masochistic passion for her:

> Madame Defarge slightly waved her hand, to imply that she heard, and might be relied upon to arrive in good time, and so went through the mud, and round the corner of the prison wall. The Vengeance and the Juryman, looking after her as she walked away, were highly appreciative of her fine figure, and her superb moral endowments.
>
> There were many women at that time, upon whom the time laid a dreadfully disfiguring hand; but, there was not one among them more to be dreaded than this ruthless woman, now taking her way along the streets. Of a strong and fearless character, of shrewd sense and readiness, of great determination, of that kind of beauty which not only seems to impart to its possessor firmness and animosity, but to strike into others an instinctive recognition of those qualities; the troubled time would have heaved her up, under any circumstances. But, imbued from her childhood with a brooding sense of wrong, and an inveterate hatred of a class, opportunity had developed her into a tigress. She was absolutely without pity. If she had ever had the virtue in her, it had quite gone out of her.
>
> It was nothing to her, that an innocent man was to die for the sins of his forefathers; she saw, not him, but them. It was nothing to her, that his wife was to be made a widow and his daughter an orphan; that was insufficient punishment, because they were her natural enemies and her prey, and as such had no right to live. To appeal to her, was made hopeless by her having no sense of pity, even for herself. If she had been laid low in the streets, in any of the many encounters in which she had been engaged, she would not have pitied herself; nor, if she had been ordered to the axe to-morrow, would she have gone to it with any softer

feeling than a fierce desire to change places with the man who sent her there.

Such a heart Madame Defarge carried under her rough robe. Carelessly worn, it was a becoming robe enough, in a certain weird way, and her dark hair looked rich under her coarse red cap. Lying hidden in her bosom, was a loaded pistol. Lying hidden at her waist, was a sharpened dagger. Thus accoutred, and walking with the confident tread of such a character, and with the supple freedom of a woman who had habitually walked in her girlhood, bare-foot and bare-legged, on the brown sea-sand, Madame Defarge took her way along the streets.

We can discount Dickens's failed ironies here ("her superb moral endowments") and his obvious and rather tiresome moral judgments upon his own creation. What comes through overwhelmingly is Dickens's desire for this sadistic woman, which is the secret of our desire for her also, and so for her nightmare power over us. "Her fine figure," "that kind of beauty . . . firmness and animosity," "a tigress . . . absolutely without pity," "a becoming robe enough, in a certain weird way," "her dark hair looked rich," "confident tread . . . supple freedom . . . bare-foot and bare-legged"—these are the stigmata of a dominatrix. Loaded pistol in her bosom, sharpened dagger at her waist, Madame Defarge is the ultimate phallic woman, a monument to fetishism, to what Freud would have called the splitting of Dickens's ego in the defensive process.

That splitting attains a triumph in the grand wrestling match, where Miss Pross, a Jacob wrestling with the Angel of Death, holds off Madame Defarge in what is supposed to be an instance of Love stronger than Death, but which is all the more effective for its sexual overtones:

Madame Defarge made at the door. Miss Pross, on the instinct of the moment, seized her round the waist in both her arms, and held her tight. It was in vain for Madame Defarge to struggle and to strike; Miss Pross, with the vigorous tenacity of love, always so much stronger than hate, clasped her tight, and even lifted her from the floor in the struggle that they had. The two hands of Madame Defarge buffeted and tore her face; but, Miss Pross, with her head down, held her round the waist, and clung to her with more than the hold of a drowning woman.

Soon, Madame Defarge's hands ceased to strike, and felt at her encircled waist. "It is under my arm," said Miss Pross, in smothered tones, "you shall not draw it. I am stronger than you, I bless Heaven for it. I'll hold you till one or other of us faints or dies!"

Madame Defarge's hands were at her bosom. Miss Pross looked up, saw what it was, struck at it, struck out a flash and a crash, and stood alone—blinded with smoke.

The embrace of Miss Pross clearly has a repressed lesbian passion for Madame Defarge in it, so that more than a transcendent love for Lucie here endows the force of the good with its immovable tenacity. But for the pistol blast, Madame Defarge would have been held until one or the other lady fainted or died. Miss Pross had never struck a blow in her life, but then her father Jacob had been no warrior either. Dickens, master of stage fire, destroyed Madame Defarge in the grand manner, the only fate worthy of so vivid and so passionately desired a creation.

The Demons of History in Dickens's *Tale*

Robert Alter

A Tale of Two Cities has probably given serious critics of Dickens more trouble than any other of his novels. Written at the height of Dickens's artistic maturity, it seems almost willfully to turn away from the very modes of imagination that had made him great and to stress some of the facile formulas that had merely made him popular. From the first, admirers of Dickens have sensed this book to be an uncharacteristic expression of his genius, while Dickens's detractors have seized upon it as a transparent revelation of his general weakness as a novelist. The novel offers good evidence for both views, though the former seems to me on the whole the more cogent of the two. On the one hand, it is clear that Dickens was attempting something new, as he himself confesses in his letters, in treating this whole historical subject. The fact, on the other hand, that the general strategy of this novel differs from that of his other fiction has the effect of leaving certain regrettable conventional elements nakedly exposed which, in the more typical novels, are submerged in the great swirl of brilliant fantastication that can only be called Dickensian. In *Little Dorrit, Bleak House, Great Expectations, Our Mutual Friend,* the teeming life of Dickensian invention tends to draw our attention away from the imaginative thinness of the heroes and heroines, the contrived coincidences, the strained notes of melodrama, the moments of dewy-eyed, lip-serving religiosity, while the more intently dramatic presentation of character and event in *A Tale of Two Cities* frequently stresses just these qualities.

The *Tale,* then, is conspicuously the uneven work of a writer

From *Motives for Fiction*. ©1984 by Robert Alter. Harvard University Press, 1984.

who, in his greatest novels as well, persists in a kind of splendid, self-transcending unevenness. It is essential, however, to try to see just what he was aiming at in this uncharacteristic book, for his peculiar method of historical fiction here does enable him to make palpable to the imagination a realm of experience that is generally beyond the scope of his other novels. If Dickens's Two Cities in the age of revolution lack the vivid humor and warmth, the intimate feel of bizarre yet familiar British experience, associated with the contemporary England of his other novels, we should not dismiss the *Tale* for failing to be another *Pickwick* but should rather seek to understand why Dickens chose to restrict the role in it of just such appealing characteristics.

The term Dickens stresses in his correspondence to distinguish the technique of the *Tale* from that of his previous novels is "picturesque," and that will do nicely for the book if we extend its meaning beyond the limited sense of "dramatic immediacy" which Dickens seems to have had in mind. Most of Dickens's fiction is boldly visual, but the visualization typically concentrates on fascinating and eccentric details, wonderful gargoyles, to borrow George Orwell's happy metaphor, rather than architectural wholes. In *A Tale of Two Cities,* on the other hand, the visual elements are deployed panoramically, often in the compositional arrangements of a large painted canvas. As nowhere else in his writing, Dickens wants to generalize his subject, and so he repeatedly holds the novel—images, characters, events—at a long distance to be seen in broad overview, its materials arranged in manifestly formal patterns. This method might well be described as picturesque, or a little more precisely, as scenic, for the *Tale* is a novel where the scene is the real event. The individual human actors are frequently no more than secondary elements of the scenes of which they are part; and the episodes that focus merely on the personages, isolated from the vivid panorama which is more often foreground than background, frequently reveal the novel at its weakest.

The novels of Dickens's maturity, as modern criticism has made abundantly clear, convey much of their meaning through the elaborate evocation of symbolic atmosphere. This is true of the *Tale* as well, but with this difference: the symbolic atmosphere does not simply give larger resonance to what happens in the novel—ultimately, it *is* what happens in the novel, for the subject as Dickens conceives it can only be represented in large symbolic terms. The plane of symbolic generalization on which the action takes place is apparent from the first paragraph. The narrator begins not with his protagonists but with the times, surveying the state of civilization in France and England in the year 1775, at once fixing the contradictions of the age in an emphatic series of formally balanced contrasts—"it was the season of Light, it was the season of Darkness, it was the spring of hope, it was the winter of despair." The capitalization of Light and Darkness, perhaps an ironic allusion to the allegorical use of such capitalized nouns in eighteenth-century English poetry, is very much to the point of the whole novel, which one could say is really "about" Light and Darkness (though chiefly the latter) in all their traditional symbolic associations.

A dank, viscous murkiness pervades the first part of the novel, and, throughout, a clouded somberness of atmosphere is sustained in the most effective scenes, where the prevailing gloom is merely accentuated by the pale inadequate glimmerings of artificial illumination or the ominous glow of violent red fires. Most of the major scenes are set at night, and there is something uncannily nocturnal even about those that supposedly take place in the light of day.

The action begins with a mail-coach making its arduous way through a clammy and impenetrable mist. When Jarvis Lorry arrives at his destination, the obscurity in the room where he meets Lucie Manette is so thick that he can scarcely make her out as he stands amidst heavy dark tables that "had been oiled and oiled, until the two tall candles on the table in the middle of the room were gloomily reflected on every leaf; as if *they* were buried, in deep graves of black mahogany, and no light to speak of could be expected from them until they were dug out." This vigorous twist of visual fantasy binds darkness and light firmly to the novel's central themes of death and resurrection, imprisonment and liberation. A few pages later, when the setting shifts to France for the first time, darkness will be more explicitly associated with the forces through which the aristocracy smothers the life of the people: in the quarter of Saint Antoine, it becomes something that can be smelled and almost touched, the dense polluted atmosphere of a "steep dark shaft of dirty and poison" that is not only the stairway to Manette's garret but also the symbolic dwelling place, the prison-house, of the poor of France.

With this accumulation of imagery, Defarge's simple statement to the crazed shoemaker-doctor in his darkened attic has a special poignancy: "I want . . . to let in a little more light here. You can bear a little more?" And the vision later of the Marquis's gloomy chateau, a single flambeau "disturbing the darkness" within it, hints at the precarious ambiguity of the relationship of darkness to light—the Marquis and his kind, by interring the people in a black prison of oppression, finally transform the people itself into a terrible force of darkness.

What Dickens is ultimately concerned with in *A Tale of Two Cities* is not a particular historical event—that is simply his chosen dramatic setting—but rather the relationship between history and evil, how violent oppression breeds violent rebellion which becomes a new kind of oppression. His account of the *ancien régime* and the French Revolution is a study in civilized man's vocation for proliferating moral chaos, and in this one important regard the *Tale* is the most compelling "modern" of his novels. He also tries hard, through the selfless devotion of his more exemplary characters, to suggest something of mankind's potential for moral regeneration; but he is considerably less convincing in this effort, partly because history itself offers so little evidence which the imagination of hope can use to sustain itself.

The most powerful imaginings of the novel reach out again and again to touch ultimate possibilities of violence, whether in the tidal waves of mass destruction or in the hideous inventiveness of individual acts of cruelty. In the first chapter we are introduced to France through the detailed description of an execution by horrible mutilation, and to England by a rapid series of images of murder, mob violence, and hangings. Throughout the novel, the English mob is in potential what the French revolutionary hordes are in bloody fact. At the English trial of the falsely accused Darnay, the "ogreish" spectators, eagerly awaiting the condemnation, vie with one another in their lip-smacking description of how a man looks being drawn and quartered. Again in France, the details of torture and savagery exercise an obscure fascination over the imagination of the characters (and perhaps of the writer as well)—nightmarish images of tongues torn out with pincers, gradual dismemberment, boiling oil and lead poured into gaping wounds, float through the darkness of the novel and linger on the retina of the memory.

The energy of destruction that gathers to such acts of concentrated horror pulses through the whole world of the novel, pounding at its foundations. It is conceived as an elemental force in nature which works through men as well. Dover Beach as Jarvis Lorry contemplates it near the beginning of the novel is a replica in nature of the revolution to come, the scene most strikingly serving as event: "the sea did what it liked, and what it liked was destruction. It thundered at the town, and thundered at the cliffs, and brought the coast down madly." The image of the revolutionary mob, much later in the novel, is simply the obverse of this vision of the ocean as chaos and darkness: "The sea of black and threatening waters, and of destructive upheaving of wave against wave, whose depths were yet unfathomed and whose forces were yet unknown. The remorseless sea of turbulently swaying shapes, voices of vengeance." These same pitiless forces are present in the rainstorm that descends upon the quiet Soho home of the Manettes as Lucie, Darnay, and Carton watch: the lightning, harbinger of revolution, that they see leaping from the stormy dark is the only light that can be born from the murky atmosphere of this world—the hot light of destruction. Later the revolution is also likened to a great earthquake, and when Madame Defarge adds to this her grim declaration—"Tell wind and fire where to stop . . . but don't tell me"—all four elements of the traditional world-picture have been associated with the forces of blind destruction, earth and water and fire and air.

There is, ultimately, a peculiar impersonality about this novel, for it is intended to dramatize the ways in which human beings become the slaves of impersonal forces, at last are made inhuman by them. In order to show the play of these elemental forces in history, Dickens adopts a generalizing novelistic technique which frequently approaches allegory, the mode of imagination traditionally used for the representation of cosmic powers doing battle or carrying out a destined plan. The Darkness and Light of the novel's first sentence are almost immediately supported by the introduction of two explicitly allegorical figures in the same chapter: the Woodman, Fate; and the Farmer, Death. In the action that follows, events and characters often assume the symbolic postures and formal masks of allegory.

The man seen clinging to the chains of the Marquis's carriage, "all covered with dust, white as a spectre, tall as a spectre," is no longer the flesh-and-blood father of the child murdered by the Marquis but has become a ghastly Messenger, sent to exact vengeance from the nobleman. The Marquis himself, always seen from an immense distance of implacable irony, is far more an allegorical representation of the French ruling classes than an individual character. The elaborate figure of a new face struck to stone by the Gorgon's head which is used to describe the Marquis's death is entirely appropriate, for his death is not a "realistic" murder but the symbolic acting out of the inexorable workings of retribution. In this novel, it is fitting that one Frenchwoman should actually be called The Vengeance, whom the narrator at the end will ironically bid by name to shout loud after a Thérèse Defarge who is forever beyond answering. It is equally fitting that Charles Darnay's

French name, Evrémonde, should sound like an English name of a different sort: he is the Everyman who is drawn to the heart of destruction, virtually gives up his life there, in legal fact and physical appearance, to be reborn only through the expiatory death of another self, and so to return to his beloved, whose name means "light."

One of the most striking symbolic tableaux in the novel, the haunting scene of the four incendiaries setting out across the countryside to burn the castles of the aristocracy, is directly modeled on a great allegory of the New Testament, for the four revolutionaries become the Four Horsemen of the Apocalypse, spreading universal ruin: "four fierce figures trudged away, east, west, north, and south, along the night-enshrouded roads, guided by the beacon they had lighted, toward their next destination." When, on the other hand, the allegory moves in from such anonymous, symbolic figures to characters with whom we are more intimately acquainted, it tends to be somewhat less successful. The fatal confrontation, for example, at the end of the novel between Miss Pross and Madame Defarge is clearly presented as a battle between pitiless French savagery and staunch English humanity ("You shall not get the better of me," says Miss Pross, "I am an Englishwoman"), between Darkness and Light, evil and good, the power of hate and the power of love. Neither combatant can understand, literally or figuratively, the language of the other, and the struggle is one to the death. One senses an obtrusive neatness here in the symmetrically symbolic roles into which the characters have been pressed: if Madame Defarge, as the exemplary Woman of the Revolution in the novel, is an appropriate champion of Darkness in this final conflict, Miss Pross is enlisted as the champion of Light only with some strain on credence. Miss Pross, of course, prevails "with the vigorous tenacity of love, always so much stronger than hate," but her victory may seem a little contrived because the novel has demonstrated the energy and tenacity of hate so much more forcefully than it has shown the power of love.

In a world dominated by vast inexorable forces, it is understandable that human action should often take the form of ritual. Ritual, after all, involves the careful repetition of a series of prescribed gestures which serve as a means of placating the inhuman powers of acting out man's fealty to them, his willing or coerced identity of purpose with them. On its lowest level, ritual expresses itself in purely obsessive action—Doctor Manette's desperate cobbling, the newly imprisoned Darnay's compulsive counting of steps. Appropriately, the obsessive ritual must be countered by a conscious ritual of exorcism: Jarvis Lorry hacks the cobbler's bench to pieces while Miss Pross holds a candle for him, and then they burn and bury the pieces, with the uneasy feeling of complicity in some terrible crime. Other ritualistic acts in the novel have a compulsive aspect, but their main purpose, as is generally the case with ritual, is broadly symbolic. The grim knitting of the wives of the Revolution, led by Madame Defarge, expresses in regular nervous motion the irresistible impulse of vengeance working within the women, and, in the allegorical scheme of the novel, it is made clear that they are the Fates, knitting an irreversible pattern of doom.

In general, Dickens's imagination of the revolutionists is founded on an insight into the religious nature of their revolutionary fervor. The faith to which they adhere is a kind of anti-Christianity, and Dickens takes pains to note that a replica of the guillotine—the symbol of unpitying vengeance—replaces the cross—the symbol of redeeming love—on every breast. This is, of course, the final balanced antithesis of Light over against Darkness in the novel. Sydney Carton, who possesses the greatest love, to lay down his life for his friend, achieves an imitation of Christ in his death, and the novel's scheme of symmetric contrasts culminates—perhaps a little too neatly—in his ascent to the scaffold, the stage of the Revolution's central rite, reciting the words of Christ, "I am the Resurrection and the Life."

Some of the most compelling scenes in this scenic novel are at once allegorical tableaux and solemn sacraments of the Revolution. The wine cask smashed outside the Defarge shop provides the opportunity for a sort of red mass in which the wine, tasted by all the people, smeared on their lips and faces, becomes blood; there is, pointedly, no bread of life—no body of Christ—for the hungry in this mass, and for that very reason the blood is solely a portent of destruction, not a promise of redemption. Much later, the ambiguity of wine and blood is recalled in another revolutionary rite, the horrendous thronging of the people to the grindstone to sharpen their blood-stained weapons, to renew themselves and their instruments for the holy purpose of slaughter.

The climactic ritual, however, in which the destructive spirit of the Revolution is celebrated, is the great frenzied dance, the Carmagnole. The movements of the dancers vividly show forth the satanic aspect of the revolutionary faith, its commitment to the elemental force of violence. Thus, the crowd of five thousand, with The Vengeance in the lead, appears before Lucie "dancing like five thousand demons . . . keeping a ferocious time that was like a gnashing of teeth in unison."

At first they seem "a mere storm" of red caps, but then Lucie sees them as "some ghastly apparition of a dance-figure gone raving mad." The dancers, that is, recapitulate scenic or symbolic events that have occurred earlier in the novel—the fierceness of the storm sweeping down on Soho, the madness of the sea pounding at Dover Beach, the various ghastly apparitions, victims of despotism and spirits of retribution alike. The Carmagnole is both an acting out of the meaning of the Revolution and a rite that inspires its celebrants with a strengthened dedication to the revolutionary cause—"a means of angering the blood, bewildering the senses, and steeling the heart." And as Dickens sums up the picture he has painted, the human figures in it are seen as representative "types"—that is, allegorical embodiments—of the movement of large forces through history: "The maidenly bosom bared to this, the pretty almost-child's head distracted, the delicate foot mincing in this slough of blood and dirt, were types of the disjointed time."

It is often claimed that the life of this novel is thin and meager because Dickens sets the major action away from the English world in which he was imaginatively at home. Quite to the contrary, it seems to me that the French scenes are the ones that really fire his imagination here, and that the most brilliantly realized character in the novel is the French revolutionary mob. The fact that a corporate entity—the many-headed monster which Dickens, like Shakespeare, saw in the mob—should so impose itself as a distinctive presence has, I think, a great deal to do with the large allegorical perspective to which the novel recurs, its habit of pulling back from the observation of particulars to see its whole subject in symbolic panorama.

The bold conception, to be sure, of an allegorical plan for the novel hardly guarantees the book's artistic success, and there is at least one very serious flaw in the execution of the plan. The symbolic conflict around which the novel is organized ultimately alludes, as I have noted, to an opposition between promised regeneration in Christ and threatened annihilation by the forces of the anti-Christ. The trouble is that while the threat of moral anarchy is as constant and close to Dickens as his own heartbeat, his imagination of resurrection, whether for individuals or for societies, is conventionally pious and little more. Nevertheless, the treatment of history in *A Tale of Two Cities* does possess a certain imaginative authority because it generally concentrates on history as the medium for the implementation of evil, which is, alas, what history has generally been, what it seems now more than ever to be.

In this connection, the emphasis placed in the novel on the idea of inevitability is worth noting. The essence of history, at least when we view it retrospectively, is inevitability, for history is before all else the record of what has already happened, which, because it has already happened, must forever be as it is and not otherwise. By dramatically translating this notion of inevitability into the irreversible progress of violence in the life of a nation, Dickens, who is usually anything but an austere writer, gives this novel a kind of oblique reflection of the stern grandeur of the Greek tragedies, where inexorable fate works itself out through human lives. "At last it is come," Defarge declares to his wife as the Revolution begins, the affirmation of an eternally destined decree ringing through his words. It is as though a law of moral physics were operating with mathematical certainty in the events of history: "Crush humanity out of shape once more, under similar hammers, and it will twist itself into the same tortured forms."

This sense of inevitability, I would suggest, is deliberately reinforced by the use of coincidence in the plot. After all, Dickens surely could have invented some credible subterfuge to get Carton into Darnay's cell without having Miss Pross discover her long-lost brother Solomon in the police-spy, Barsad, at the crucial moment, without the superfluous abundance of evidence against Barsad in the testimonies of Mr. Lorry, Carton himself, and even Jerry Cruncher, all conveniently present just when needed. In compounding the initial coincidence of physical similarity between Darnay and Carton with all these other coincidences, Dickens demonstrates not only his own habitual delight in mystification and manipulation but also how the lines of destiny imperceptibly converge on a single, inevitable point—in this case, the scaffold of the guillotine, where Sydney Carton will take the place of Charles Darnay on the day when fifty-two heads have been appointed to roll, as surely as there are fifty-two weeks in the fixed annual cycle.

Against this background of inexorable destiny, the "happy ending" of A Tale of Two Cities includes an element of unillusioned realism absent from the conclusions to Dickens's other books. In the world of this novel, expiation must be made—the phrase is invoked at the climax of Carton's final prophecy—both by individuals and by nations. The aristocracy must pay the price of the iniquities it has perpetrated, and the revolutionaries will pay the price of their own terrible violence. Charles Darnay, descendant of the Evrémondes, must die in the Place of the Revolution, if only vicariously, through his double. Nobody gets off scot-free from the encounter with history:

curiously, a price is even exacted from the innocent Miss Pross for her conquest of Madame Defarge; the pistol-shot that destroys Thérèse Defarge leaves Miss Pross stone-deaf till her dying day.

I have been emphasizing how Dickens visualized history in a more or less ordered symbolic scheme, but it is important to add that his visualization reaches moments of intensity which have to be called visionary. Dickens, as criticism in the past two decades has amply recognized, was a hallucinated genius, fascinated and bedeviled by the imagined persons and events cast up from the depths of his own inner world. When he speaks in the preface to the *Tale* of the "complete possession" the book had over him while he wrote it, he uses that term in the sense of possession by spirits, or demons. What he says of the unforgettable vision of the revolutionary mob at the grindstone could easily be extended to his entire recreation of history in the novel: "All this was seen in a moment, as the vision of a drowning man, or of any human creature at any very great pass, could see a world as if it were there." Dickens in his mature years was in his own emotional life a drowning man, fiercely refusing to go under, creating out of his increasingly pained sense of life great and sometimes still exuberant fiction through a heroic exertion of will. In *A Tale of Two Cities* the drowning man's vision achieves piercing moments of prophetic comprehensiveness because it is focused on history itself and on the vast moral struggle he saw implicit in history. Whatever the faults of the book, there is still much in it that can speak to us in the very great pass to which our own history has come, with its recurrent premonitions of a universal drowning.

The Carlylean Vision
of *A Tale of Two Cities*

David D. Marcus

A Tale of Two Cities is the most disparaged and least understood of
Dickens's late novels. Overwhelmingly, the critics have judged the
work a failure and dismissed it as intellectually superficial. According
to this view, Dickens held only the most simpleminded view of history, and although the novel fictionalizes events whose memory haunted
the Victorian era, it never places those events in the context of a
coherent understanding of the processes of social change; the book is
an amalgam of romantic melodrama based on Dickens's experience as
an actor in Wilkie Collins's *Frozen Deep* and fragments taken from
Carlyle's *French Revolution,* a work from which Dickens unsystematically
borrowed details but not any conceptual framework. Thus understood, the novel splits in two; its connection between romance and the
French Revolution seems tenuous and contrived. As Georg Lukács
complains, "neither the fate of Manette and his daughter, nor of
Darnay-Evrémonde, the least of all of Sidney Carton, grows organically out of the age and its social events." Taylor Stoehr's very different approach to the novel also admits this split by disregarding Dickens's
political ideas and interpreting the historical events as a ritual expiation
through violence for the sexual violation that is the original cause of
the action.

But in fact, the two plots are closely related, and that relationship
points toward a much more complex vision of history than criticism
has so far allowed. My discussion of this relationship will also suggest

From *Studies in the Novel* 8, no. 1 (Spring 1976). © 1976 by North Texas State
University.

that Dickens's conceptual debt to Carlyle is much greater than recent criticism has recognized. Dickens and Carlyle share a common quest that informs the historical vision of *A Tale of Two Cities*: both writers seek ways in which people can socialize their energies in an age whose institutions seem at odds with any humanly valuable purpose. Dickens's exploration of revolutionary France resembles Teufelsdröckh's spiritual pilgrimage in *Sartor Resartus* and the exhortatory social criticism of *Past and Present* in the connection that it draws between the social and the psychic dimensions of historical crisis; the humane man finds himself caught in the mechanism of historical processes that move according to their own laws and that destroy any possibility of useful action. It is precisely this tie between the social and the psychic that unites the romantic and revolutionary plots of *A Tale of Two Cities*.

As Robert Alter has noted of the novel's French episodes, they are "intended to dramatize the ways in which human beings become the slaves of impersonal forces, at last are made inhuman by them." But the English as well as the French episodes deal with the problem of historical dehumanization. At the end of the novel, Darnay and Dr. Manette retreat into the tranquillity of a secluded domestic circle, and that retreat has to be seen in the light of their failure as public men to influence the course of events. Thus their retreat and the quasi-religious redemption through love and self-sacrifice are actually strategies for coping with the characters' need to find a sense of fruitful relatedness in the face of the impossibility of solving social problems. For Dickens, the family and religion serve much the same function as religion and the corporate spirit did for Carlyle: they are means of humanizing the void left in the individual life by mechanistic social institutions.

In describing the relationship between Carlyle and Dickens, I am emphasizing the social and secular sides of Carlyle's works and his role as the interpreter of the Romantic tradition to Victorian England. In commenting on Carlyle's phrase "natural supernaturalism," M. H. Abrams has said of the Romantic era that "the general tendency was, in diverse degrees and ways to naturalize the supernatural and to humanize the divine" (*Natural Supernaturalism: Tradition and Revolution in Romantic Literature*). Certainly this description applies to Carlyle himself; for all of his explicitly religious interpretation of experience, the end result even in *Sartor Resartus* is a reorientation of the individual that allows him to experience a sense of purpose in his work. As George Levine has pointed out, Carlyle's contemporaries as well as many later readers saw Teufelsdröckh's spiritual pilgrimage as a call for "a moral and social as well as a religious revolution" (*The Boundaries of Fiction: Carlyle, Macauley, Newman*). Whether Carlyle is historically the only source of Dickens's efforts at dealing with the problem of the individual's relationship to his culture is not strictly demonstrable, although Dickens's own sense of himself as a disciple of Carlyle's certainly lends an air of plausibility to such speculation. But Carlyle did crystallize these problems for his age, and both men saw the crisis of their culture in similar terms. Thus Carlyle provides at the very least a useful model for understanding Dickens, and for seeing Dickens as the heir to the Romantic era's tendency to internalize historical phenomena. Like Carlyle and the Romantic poets, Dickens is concerned with defining the possibilities for self-fulfillment in a society whose institutions seem inimical to all that is distinctively human.

From the beginning of *A Tale of Two Cities,* Dickens concentrates on the difficulty of understanding public events for those immersed in them. The famous opening paragraph presents the reader with a series of neat antitheses that in sum offer confusion rather than clarity:

> It was the best of times, it was the worst of times, it was the age of wisdom, it was the age of foolishness, it was the age of belief, it was the epoch of incredulity, it was the season of Light, it was the season of Darkness, it was the spring of hope, it was the winter of despair, we had everything before us, we had nothing before us, we were all going direct to heaven, we were all going direct the other way—in short, the period was so far like the present period, that some of its noisiest authorities insisted on its being received, for good or for evil, in the superlative degree of comparison only.

At first, this passage seems to be a direct authorial commentary, but the attribution of these extreme opinions to some of the age's "noisiest authorities" invites us to question whether the noisiest and most extreme authorities of any age are to be trusted. The patterned rhetoric of the passage reveals confusion rather than understanding. The difficulties of reaching any clear knowledge of one's own era emerge through the novelist's explicit comparison of the past to the present and through the irony that both history and the novelist lend to the eighteenth-century's view of itself: "In both countries [England and France] it was clearer than crystal to the lords of the State preserves of loaves and fishes, that things in general were settled for ever" (bk. 1, chap. 1). As Dickens points out immediately afterwards, the year is 1775, and with both the American and French Revolutions impending, things in general are anything but settled forever. As the novel's first paragraph makes clear, both the age's noisiest authorities and its powers that be are unaware of the significance of the historical forces that are shaping the future.

Only in retrospect do events assume a clear order. The novel's French episodes invite the reader to view every incident in the light of his historical knowledge and to recognize events as pieces in a larger pattern that is known a priori. All of the French action appears first as a foreshadowing and later as a realization of the Revolution, and Dickens eschews subtlety in favor of a directness that always keeps before the reader the relationship of each action to larger historical forces. Thus the opening French scene with its broken wine cask flooding the street suggests in its sacramental overtones the blood that will one day flow in the streets; but Dickens is not content to leave matters at the level of suggestion: "The time was to come, when that wine too would be spilled on the street-stones, and when the stain of it would be red upon many there" (bk. 1, chap. 5). Taylor Stoehr's rhetorical analysis of this and succeeding French episodes very thoroughly points out the linguistic methods through which Dickens creates a strong sense of the links among all of these events. Even the novel's web of closely interrelated characters is only a transformation of French historical forces into personal terms.

Similarly, the French characters have no individuality but exist only to play their roles in the revolutionary drama. They are defined exclusively in terms of their class. Our first glimpse of the Marquis is at a reception at which he is singled out only after a very Carlylean critique of a degenerate aristocracy whose only function has become self-aggrandizement: "Military officers destitute of military knowledge; naval officers with no idea of a ship; civil officers without a notion of affairs; brazen ecclesiastics, of the worst world worldly . . . all totally unfit for their several callings, all lying horribly in pretending to belong to them, but all nearly or remotely of the order of Monseigneur, and therefore foisted on all public employments" (bk. 2, chap. 7). Although the marquis is out of Monseigneur's favor, he is nevertheless the perfect aristocrat: he can respond to others only in terms of their class and recognizes no common bonds of humanity. His carriage kills a child, and he can see the event only in terms of his contempt for the poor: "I would ride over any of you very willingly, and exterminate you from the earth" (bk. 2, chap. 7). To his nephew

Charles Darnay, he laments the deterioration of the power of the aristocracy: "Our not remote ancestors held the right of life and death over the surrounding vulgar" (bk. 2, chap. 9). The Marquis despises Darnay for his humane feelings. And of course, there are the events related in Dr. Manette's prison diary in which the Marquis and his brother destroy a peasant family in order to exercise their *droit du seigneur*.

If the French Revolution is a form of retribution for such distortions of humanity, it is also paradoxically a continuation of them; the new order merely perpetuates the dehumanizing class-consciousness of the old. Just as the Marquis and the society he represents were trapped within a system that allowed them to perceive others only in terms of their position within the social system, so too are the revolutionaries trapped within their own inversion of that system. Charles Darnay's journey into France most clearly dramatizes how little the overthrow of the old institutions has changed the premises behind French society's judgments of human beings. As he prepares to leave England, Darnay comforts himself with the belief that his renunciation of his social position and his efforts to assist his impoverished tenants will protect him (bk. 2, chap. 24); but the reader, who has seen the condemnation of the Evrémonde race by Defarge and his fellow conspirators, recognizes that Darnay's very reasonable point of view is a misunderstanding, a projection of his own humanity into a very inhumane situation. To the new order, Darnay can be nothing more than the representative of a doomed aristocratic family.

One's position as a citizen subsumes all other ties, and revolutionary France has as little respect as the late Marquis for the feelings that bind families together. Dr. Manette's belief that his suffering now has value as a means of saving his son-in-law from the guillotine proves an illusion; the Revolution is unconcerned with the purely personal. The populace has revived the "questionable public virtues of antiquity," so that the President of the court that is about to condemn Darnay draws cheers from the crowd by telling Dr. Manette "that the good physician of the Republic would deserve better still of the Republic by rooting out an obnoxious family of Aristocrats, and would doubtless feel a sacred glow and joy in making his daughter a widow and her child an orphan" (bk. 3, chap. 10). Madame Defarge plots to destroy the remaining members of the Evrémonde family—Lucie, her child, and Dr. Manette—by using their human feelings against them; she is going to accuse them of grieving for Darnay, and in revolutionary France even grief is subject to legal regulation: mourning for a victim of the guillotine is itself a capital offense (bk. 3, chap. 12).

Dickens emphasizes the inhumanity of the French Revolution not merely for sentimental reasons but as a means of distinguishing social upheaval from substantive change. On the one hand, social upheaval comes about as the inevitable result of oppression and exploitation. As the tumbrils roll through the streets of Paris toward the guillotine, Dickens gives a direct warning: "Crush humanity out of shape once more, under similar hammers, and it will twist itself into the same tortured forms" (bk. 3, chap. 15). On the other hand, substantive change can occur only when people discard the "mind-forg'd manacles" within which they are trapped, the state of mind that remains long after the external exploiters and oppressors have been destroyed. Of course, such change can occur only within the individual, but that is not to say that Dickens is naive: for if the true instrument of oppression is a state of mind, what possible institutional solution is there? Dickens's lack of faith in political action and the inward direction of his social criticism is more than the Victorian fear of revolution. He is the heir to the inward turning that took place in Wordsworth and Coleridge in the wake of the failure of their faith in the French Revolution. As Carlyle counseled his readers in *Past and Present,*

> It were infinitely handier if we had a Morrison's Pill, Act of Parliament, or remedial measure, which men could swallow, one good time, and then go on in their old courses, cleared from all miseries and mischiefs! Unluckily we have none such; unluckily the Heavens themselves, in their rich pharmacopoeia, contain none such. There will no "thing" be done that will cure you. There will a radical universal alteration of your regimen and way of life take place; there will a most agonizing divorce between you and your chimeras, luxuries and falsities, take place . . . that so the inner fountains of life may again begin, like eternal Light-fountains, to irradiate and purify your bloated, swollen, fouler existence, drawing nigh, as at present, to nameless death.

Without such an inner transformation, the new order in France can only perpetuate the old oppression by continuing the inherited class-based assumptions about what human beings are. For Dickens, revolution is institutional, but change is psychic.

The religious transformation that takes place within Sidney Carton illustrates both this concern for the inner life of the individual as the only possible means of change and Dickens's use of religious motifs as a way of talking about that inner life. As Carton stands at the guillotine ready to die, he has, according to the observers that Dickens places at the scene, "the peacefullest man's face ever beheld there" (bk. 3, chap 15). He is in the grip of a prophetic vision, one that even offers him a form of redemption through Lucie's as yet unborn child: "I see that child who lay upon her bosom and who bore my name, a man winning his way up in that path of life which once was mine. I see him winning it so well, that my name is made illustrious there by the light of his. I see the blots I threw upon it, faded away" (bk. 3, chap. 15). But Carton's vision secularizes the religious theme of immortality by substituting the continuity of generations for religious mystery. There is no suggestion that he will survive in any other sense; he refers to his coming death as a "far, far better rest . . . than I have ever known" (bk. 3, chap. 15). Carton's vision simply asserts the newfound sense of relatedness that has led him to sacrifice his life; he now feels himself linked by human ties to a future that he will not personally see. He is no longer the "disappointed drudge" who cares for no one and is cared for by no one (bk. 2, chap. 4). The spirit of optimism in his prophecy arises not out of a faith in God but from a faith in the best that men can become.

The novel's religious symbols follow this pattern: they reflect human attitudes and actions within social boundaries rather than a teleology. Dickens strips religion of any necessary connection with God so that it becomes simply the human potential for good or ill, for the loving self-sacrifice of a Sidney Carton or the indiscriminate destruction of the French revolutionaries. Religious feeling at its best now functions as a basis for human community, a way in which men can reach beyond themselves, experience a sense of fruitful relatedness, and grow beyond the loneliness that many other Victorian writers— Marx, Mill, Arnold, and especially Carlyle—describe as a universal malady of their age. But Dickens recognizes that this positive relatedness is only one possible recasting of Christianity in human terms. The fury of the Carmagnole—"a something once innocent, delivered over to all devilry" (bk. 3, chap. 5)—is another form of community; the Cross can also be transformed into the guillotine: "It was the sign of the regeneration of the human race. It superseded the Cross. Models of it were worn on breasts from which the cross was discarded, and it was bowed down to and believed in where the Cross was denied" (bk. 3, chap. 4). In popular mythology, the French now worship St. Guillotine "for the great sharp female was by that time popularly canonised" (bk. 3, chap. 5). Thus in France, the redefinition of religious faith precludes those human values that have been traditionally associated with Christianity. As an enraged mob finally hangs the hated Foulon on a lamppost after repeated failure, the author remarks "then, the rope was merciful," a pointed reminder of the virtue that is lacking in the mob (bk. 2, chap. 22).

Similarly, as Robert Alter points out, the four incendiaries who burn the Marquis's chateau suggest the four horsemen of the apocalypse. We do not, however, have the biblical apocalypse, but a fear that the death of the old order may also be a foreshadowing of the death of all order. The one incendiary Dickens describes at length appears in the midst of a barren, unproductive landscape and is ominously portrayed as "a shaggy-haired man, of almost barbarian aspect" (bk. 2, chap. 23). As he sleeps, the reader comes to see him through the eyes of the road-mender who is the sole observer within the scene:

> Stooping down beside him, the road-mender tried to get a peep at secret weapons in his breast or where not; but, in vain, for he slept with his arms crossed upon him, and set as resolutely as his lips. Fortified towns with their stockades, guard-houses, gates, trenches, and drawbridges, seemed to the mender of roads, to be so much air as against this figure. And when he lifted his eyes from it to the horizon and looked around, he saw in his small fancy similar figures, stopped by no obstacle, tending to centres all over France.
>
> (bk. 2, chap. 23)

In each sentence, Dickens reminds us that this vision of destruction is taking place within the mind of the road-mender. Apocalypse thus acquires a social meaning in two ways: it figures the widespread devastation that actually takes place within France, but it also conveys the consciousness of that devastation, the disappearance of any faith in the stability of things. Historically and psychically, the symbolism of apocalypse is, like the symbolism of the guillotine, an inversion of tradition that leaves only the horror with none of the hope.

English society, by contrast, does offer some hope, although of a very limited sort. Dickens creates a number of similarities between Britain and France, similarities that undermine any self-satisfied confidence in the inherent superiority of British institutions and attitudes.

England has no special historical foresight as the references to the American Revolution in the opening chapter and at Darnay's trial make clear (bk. 2, chap. 3). Dickens also suggests that the English have a potential for violence very like that of the French. He labels the crowd at Darnay's English trial "ogreish" in its interest (bk. 2, chap. 2). And the spectator who describes "with a relish" the gruesome penalty for high treason (bk. 2, chap. 2) is as much the connoisseur of death as Jacques Three who contemplates "like an epicure" his vision of Lucie and her daughter in the hands of the executioner (bk. 3, chap. 14). The mob that turns the supposed funeral of John Barsad, the spy, into a near riot palely but surely echoes the grotesque French mobs that dance wildly through the streets of Paris. And like both the French monarchy and the revolutionaries who succeed it, the English law indiscriminately employs the services of the executioner who can be seen "to-day taking the life of an atrocious murderer, and to-morrow of a wretched pilferer who had robbed a farmer's boy of six-pence" (bk. 1, chap. 1).

But in England, unlike France, it is impossible to see all events as parts of a pattern. Much to everyone's surprise, Charles Darnay is acquitted in England. Moreover, there is a disjunction between public and private life. Despite his assurances that he is "a mere machine" in the service of Tellson's (bk. 1, chap. 4), Mr. Lorry does develop an emotionally rich personal existence through his acquaintance with the Manette family. In contrast to the French scenes that show the relationships of people to one another and to the events around them as controlled by the pattern of French history, the early English scenes emphasize the uncertainty of both the reader's and the character's perceptions and how little the characters know of one another. As Mr. Lorry rides toward Dover, Dickens tells us that the coach "was in its usual genial position that the guard suspected the passengers, the passengers suspected one another and the guard, they all suspected everybody else, and the coachman was sure of nothing but the horses" (bk. 1, chap. 2). The passengers keep themselves so separated from one another that at Darnay's English trial, Mr. Lorry is unable to say—and indeed we never learn—whether Darnay was in the coach. As Jerry Cruncher returns to London bearing Mr. Lorry's cryptic message, the narrator meditates on human isolation and concludes with a rhetorical question: "In any of the burial-places of this city through which I pass, is there a sleeper more inscrutable than its busy inhabitants are, in their innermost personality, to me, or than I am to them?" (bk. 1, chap. 3).

In England, there are limitations on one's ability to perceive, and in sharp contrast to France, the reader is no longer able to place data in context, to see the coherence of events.

Dickens treats this secrecy that shrouds every individual with characteristic ambivalence. The early coach scenes portray a social atmosphere of constant distrust and fragmentation; as Dickens tells us, "the highwayman in the dark was a City tradesman in the light" (bk. 1, chap. 1). The example of Jerry Cruncher makes abundantly clear that one's private existence is not necessarily a haven in which domestic virtue flourishes. Moreover, the narrator's commentary on the inability of people to know one another implies a loneliness that is developed more fully in the portrait of Sidney Carton. But for all these limitations, the possibility of a private identity has the great advantage of making England a culture in which personality can be multidimensional, in which the publicly visible self is but one part.

In such a society, the individual can think of himself and others in a variety of contradictory terms, and this process of conflict allows the individual to change. This most clearly takes place in the tensions that beset Dr. Manette. At his first appearance in the novel, he is a man completely stripped of his identity by the ordeal of his imprisonment; he works quietly at his shoemaking and passively submits to others. But after a period in England, another side of his personality dominates, a side that completely reverses the passivity of the prisoner: "He was now a very energetic man indeed, with great firmness of purpose, strength of resolution, and vigour of action" (bk. 2, chap. 10). This reversal of his personality does not mean that he has escaped the past, for he continues to bear the prisoner within him. At crucial moments, he reverts or attempts to revert to his shoemaking: when he suspects Darnay's true identity (bk. 2, chap. 10), when he finally learns it (bk. 2, chap. 17), and when he ultimately feels himself responsible for Darnay's condemnation by the revolutionary tribunal (bk. 3, chap. 12). Doctor Manette is able to accept Darnay and to recover from his ordeal because he thinks of himself not only as the wronged prisoner but as Lucie's father. As Darnay hints of his actual descent, the doctor responds that if there are "any fancies, any reasons, any apprehensions, anything whatsoever, new or old, against the man she really loved— the direct responsibility thereof not lying on his head—they should all be obliterated for her sake" (bk. 2, chap. 10). As the doctor's final relapse makes clear, that obliteration is an incomplete process, but he is able to achieve a new inner balance in which the old wrongs are outweighed by his love for his daughter.

Such change has effects that are felt only within the sphere of immediate relationships. It is not the result of dedication to great causes but of following the injunction that Carlyle borrowed from Goethe: *"Do the Duty which lies nearest thee."* Thus Sidney Carton finds a sense of purposefulness through his devotion to Lucie to whom he has said "For you, and for any dear to you, I would do anything" (bk. 2, chap. 13). Like Dr. Manette, Carton exemplifies the contradictory possibilities inherent in human nature. He has told Darnay after the courtroom scene of this sense of emotional isolation (bk. 2, chap. 4), and he tells Lucie, "I am like one who died young. All my life might have been" (bk. 2, chap. 13). But as he walks through Paris with his mind set on sacrificing himself to help Lucie and her family, a sense of relatedness returns; he remembers his father's funeral, and the words of the burial service pass through his mind (bk. 3, chap. 9). And his changed state appears to the very last not only in the dramatic act of dying in the place of another but also in the kindness that he displays toward the seamstress who precedes him to the guillotine. Carton's love for Lucie has aroused the sympathetic capacity within his nature, and by caring for another, he finally emerges from the self-imposed prison of indifference. He is finally able to respond to those around him.

Clearly Dickens is not giving us any formula for the regeneration of the human race; the most radical effect that individual change brings about is reconciliation within families. This emphasis on intimate relationships does imply a view of society, but that view is largely negative: the individual must not be excessively burdened by his social identity, he must have room to develop with the contradictory fullness that is distinctively human. But even within a culture that offers that possibility, society does not offer any encouragement to the best human impulses. If Doctor Manette is recalled to life from the grave of his imprisonment, John Barsad parodies that same theme in his mock funeral and reappearance in France as precisely what he has always been, a spy. If Charles Darnay uses the freedom from the past that England offers him to make a new and productive life, Sidney Carton, the character who so uncannily resembles Darnay, is too paralyzed to realize either his emotional or professional capabilities except in his final self-sacrifice. The love of Lucie Manette acts as a regenerative force, but not all women have that power. Miss Pross maintains an unquestioning loyalty to her brother, a loyalty that has no effect other than relieving her of all her property, and Jerry Cruncher remains through most of the book insensible to his wife's prayers. Lucie is clearly a force for the good, but the French episodes, with their portrait of the bloodthirsty Madame Defarge and her companions, effectively undercut any notion that Dickens uncritically idealizes women as moral forces. In *A Tale of Two Cities,* no external circumstance can do more than create an atmosphere in which change is possible; the individual's readiness is all.

A Tale of Two Cities does not pose domesticity and religion as remedies for the great social problems of the nineteenth century; at most, Dickens's versions of faith and family offer the individual some refuge from the void left by the futility of public action. For whatever solutions Dickens offers are given with the same awareness that is the basis of Carlyle's social criticism: the old clothes of society—its beliefs, its institutions, its politics—are worn out and no longer fill human needs. Thus the novel's tale of private romance becomes a confession of public despair. At the end of the book, the characters retreat into domesticity only after both Darnay and Dr. Manette have tried to influence the course of public events and have clearly failed. Institutions seem impervious to human effort: good men waste their lives if they engage in activism. What Dickens can do on a miniature scale—redefine traditional institutions so that a small group can be based on human values—he cannot do for his culture. Like the author of *Sartor Resartus,* Dickens recognized the death of the old world but could not visualize the birth of a new.

Certainly as so many critics have claimed, this novel leaves the reader dissatisfied, and part of that dissatisfaction is rooted in Dickens's tendency toward facile moralizing. But the novel also deliberately engenders dissatisfaction through its presentation of the extreme disparity between public and private life. Institutions exist not only as social mechanisms but also through the states of mind they create within their culture, and to destroy the mechanisms cannot in itself bring about substantive change. The old order in France had created a society of unidimensional men who in the overthrow of the past could not break away from the enslaving spirit of their history. The French Revolution abolishes the monarchy, abolishes the aristocracy, abolishes the financial exploiters, but in its perverse way, it embodies the values of these traditional oppressors.

The malaise that Dickens sees in the French Revolution is characteristic of his anatomy of society in his late novels. *A Tale of Two Cities* presents in its most extreme form the same inability to translate private virtue into public action that in other novels plagues English society; the Circumlocution Office in *Little Dorrit* and the Court of Chancery in *Bleak House* poison the will of Englishmen. These institutions work according to their own internal logic and not to fulfill any human need, and as Daniel Doyce and Richard Carstone learn, they dehumanize anyone who comes into contact with them. Such institutions respond to nothing outside of themselves. It is better, Dickens says, to retreat into a sphere of a few close relationships where action becomes meaningful, to make one's garden grow; but whatever hope Dickens offers for private life grows out of an acceptance of social despair.

Unlike Dickens, Carlyle seems to offer some hope that the process by which men change themselves and dedicate their energies to the fulfillment of their immediate duties can perhaps in the long run transform society. It is likely that this hope struck a responsive note in his contemporaries and brought Carlyle to the height of his popularity in the late 1830s and the 1840s. It is also probably the extinction of that hope that brought to the fore Carlyle's more authoritarian tendencies and that to some degree alienated him from a part of his audience. But the differences between Carlyle and Dickens should not obscure the basic similarity of their outlooks: both writers believe that man's self-realization can occur only in a social context and yet that contact with society is inherently destructive. Like Wordsworth and Coleridge in the aftermath of the French Revolution, both Carlyle and Dickens are seeking a means by which people can experience a sense of purposeful action in a society whose institutions are devoid of all human purpose and whose populace has come to reflect that inhumanity.

Nation and Generation in *A Tale of Two Cities*

Albert D. Hutter

> *It is the interplay of the personal and the social, of the individual psychic development and the general political and economic evolution—with each "causing" and influencing the other . . . —that makes for the powerful social change that we call history.*
>
> BRUCE MAZLISH, *James and John Stuart Mill*

Two revolutions, one generational and the other political, determine the structure of *A Tale of Two Cities.* We require a combination of critical methods—literary, psychoanalytic, historical—to illuminate the novel's complex structure and its impact on different readers. Lee Sterrenburg writes that Dickens's vision of the French Revolution may be influenced by "a personal daydream only he can fully fathom. But he is able to communicate with his readers because he has rendered his daydream in terms of a publicly meaningful iconography." Since *A Tale of Two Cities* is also a tale of two generations, the iconography of father-son conflict carries a particularly powerful social resonance.

Dickens's novel was published in 1859, a year that Asa Briggs calls a "turning point" in the "late Victorian revolt against authority." This revolt originated "in mid-Victorian society. What happened inside families then influenced what happened in many areas of public life later" (*Victorian People*). The major publications of 1859, from *The Origin of Species* and Marx's *Critique of Political Economy* to Samuel Smiles's *Self-Help,* stand poised between the anticipation of a later ideological revolt and the still-powerful memory of the French Revolution. That revolution and subsequent English social reform inevitably

From *PMLA* 93, no. 3 (May 1978). © 1978 by the Modern Language Association of America.

changed Victorian father-son relations. But the changing Victorian family, in turn, reshaped society. As much as any other work of 1859, *A Tale of Two Cities* demonstrates the correlation between family and nation, and it uses the language of psychological conflict and psychological identification to portray social upheaval and the restoration of social order.

Nation and generation converge in the earliest chronological event of *A Tale of Two Cities,* Doctor Manette's story of the Evrémondes' brutality (bk. 3, chap. 10). The Evrémondes rape a young peasant girl, wound her brother, then summon Manette to treat their victims. When Manette tries to report these crimes, he is incarcerated in the Bastille. He writes a full account of his experience—damning the Evrémondes to the last of their race—and hides this personal history in his cell. Defarge finds the document and uses it as evidence against Charles Darnay, né Evrémonde. The events Manette describes, a microcosm of the larger narrative, trigger the major actions and reversals of the double plot. The rape itself implies social exploitation, a classwide droit du seigneur. Conversely, one peasant's attack on his master anticipates the nation's reply to such abuse. The Evrémonde who raped the girl and murdered her brother will later run down a small child from the Paris slums, and as a result will be "driven fast to his tomb." The retaliation denied one peasant, a generation earlier, is carried out by the revolutionary "Jacques." Even the Paris tribunal at which Manette's story is read reflects a struggle between parents and children: Manette has condemned his son-in-law to death.

Class conflict here reveals a hidden psychological conflict that recurs throughout the novel. Manette is taken at night and forced to witness the aftermath of a violent sexual assault. His abductors have absolute power, and any knowledge of their activities carries grave risk: "The things that you see here," the Marquis warns young Manette, "are things to be seen, and not spoken of" (bk. 3, chap. 10). Violence and sexuality, combined with a mysterious nocturnal setting and a dangerous observation, suggest a primal scene. Such scenes arouse anxiety about being caught spying, and they invariably reflect parent-child conflict. The political significance of this drama intensifies its psychological meaning. Evrémonde's absolute power, for example, resembles the father's absolute power over his child. The novel's virtual obsession with spying, its comic subplot, and its descriptions of revolutionary violence all further suggest primal-scene fantasies. But if we mistake this primal-scene reading for a full explanation of the novel, we only succeed in isolating one meaning and subordinating the others. We could as easily argue that the dominant class struggle—not simply in the novel but in Victorian history—is being expressed through the powerful language of childhood trauma: the nation is symbolized by the family; a national and historical struggle is made particular, and particularly vivid, through a personal and psychological narrative. The two explanations are not mutually exclusive. But to integrate them we must first analyze the whole work and locate the reader's experience in the structure of the text itself. It can be shown that the psychological chronology of the *Tale*'s plot, turning as it does on Manette's story, duplicates a psychological chronology common to the experience of most readers.

Manette's story is the narrative equivalent of a trauma: it recalls an event that precedes all the other action of the novel and organizes that action, although it is not "recovered" until quite late in the novel. Modern psychoanalytic theory recognizes the retrospective quality of trauma, the way in which the individual reconstructs his past life to conform with present conflicts and thereby invests a past event with significance—some of it real, often some of it imagined. Manette's document stands in a similar relationship to the larger novel: within the structure of the *Tale* it acts like a traumatic memory, reliving the significant antecedent events of the entire plot at the climax of Darnay's second trial. The document reveals the combination of public and private acts that informs the narrative; it records the "primal scene" of the text itself.

Because Dickens makes this document the hidden nexus of the plot, it must bear a considerable weight of coincidence. The abused peasants are the brother and sister of Madame Defarge; Ernest Defarge was originally Doctor Manette's servant; and Manette, before being rushed off to the Bastille, even meets his future son-in-law. Manette is sought out by the Marquise St. Evrémonde, who has "a presentiment that if no other innocent atonement is made" for the wrongdoing of her husband and brother-in-law, "it will one day be required" of little Charles (bk. 3, chap. 10)—a prophecy as remarkable as any of the "spiritual revelations" satirized by Dickens in the first chapter.

Like the story of Doctor Manette, the larger action of the novel turns on seeing what was never meant to be seen, an experience symbolized by the extensive use of a "Gorgon's Head." This mythical figure, which turned those who looked at it into stone, is now itself a "stone face [which] seemed to stare amazed, and, with opened mouth and dropped under-jaw, looked awe-stricken" (bk. 2, chap. 9). The novel begins by opposing things hidden and things revealed. The passengers on the Dover Mail "were wrapped to the cheek-bones and over the ears, and wore jack-boots. Not one of the three could have said, from anything he saw, what either of the other two was like; and each was hidden under almost as many wrappers from the eyes of the mind, as from the eyes of the body, of his two companions" (bk. 1, chap. 2). And we are repeatedly aware of eyes, hundreds of eyes, at critical moments in the text, such as Darnay's appearance at his London trial:

> Everybody present . . . stared at him . . . Eager faces strained round pillars and corners, to get a sight of him; spectators in back rows stood up, not to miss a hair of him; people on the floor of the court, laid their hands on the shoulders of the people before them, to help themselves, at anybody's cost, to a view of him—stood a-tiptoe, got upon ledges, stood upon next to nothing, to see every inch of him.
>
> (bk. 2, chap. 2)

At Darnay's second Paris trial, Dickens halts the action by a momentary frieze of staring spectators:

> In a dead silence and stillness—the prisoner under trial looking lovingly at his wife, his wife only looking from him to look with solicitude at her father, Doctor Manette keeping his eyes fixed on the reader, Madame Defarge never taking hers from the prisoner, Defarge never taking his from his feasting wife, and all the other eyes there intent upon the Doctor, who saw none of them—the paper was read, as follows.
>
> (bk. 3, chap. 9)

The novel is filled with spies, from a hero twice accused of spying, to the comic spying of Jerry Cruncher, Jr., on his father, to the spy Barsad and "the great brotherhood of Spies" (bk. 2, chap. 22) who inhabit St. Antoine. Even the dead men, their heads on Temple Bar, remind us of "the horror of being ogled" (bk. 2, chap. 1). And the novel closes with an obsessive parade of violence, the revolutionaries worshiping the guillotine and previewing its victims at mass trials.

Spying, like virtually everything else in this novel, has two meanings—one public, the other private. The official spies, like Barsad, are instruments of repression and representatives of the "fathers," the men of power. But in other contexts, like the Cruncher scenes, children spy on their parents. In both cases spying expresses the *Tale*'s dominant conflicts. Thus the Gorgon's Head witnesses much more than the murder of the Marquis: it sees the deadly struggle between two generations, which is climaxed by implicit filicide and patricide. Dickens anticipates the public murders of the Revolution while suggesting the private conflict of Charles Darnay through the subtle mixture of two plot lines. First, the Marquis—Charles's uncle, who is virtually indistinguishable from Charles's father ("Can I separate my father's twin-brother, joint inheritor, and next successor, from himself?" (bk. 2, chap. 9)—runs down a child (bk. 2, chap. 7). When the Marquis returns home, the child's avenger clings to the underpart of the Marquis's carriage (bk. 2, chap. 8). The Marquis is vaguely uneasy when he learns that someone was seen hanging from his carriage, but by the end of the chapter his thoughts have shifted to his nephew. He inquires whether Charles has arrived and is informed "not yet." Early in the next chapter, the Marquis believes he sees a shadow outside his window as he is eating, but the servants find nothing. And again, his vague uneasiness is replaced by an uneasiness over the arrival of his renegade nephew. Dickens's description encourages us to feel one preoccupation merge with the other:

> "Monseigneur, it is nothing. The trees and the night are all that are here."
> . . . the Marquis went on with his supper. He was halfway through it, when he again stopped with his glass in his hand, hearing the sound of wheels. It came on briskly, and came up to the front of the château.
> "Ask who is arrived."
> It was the nephew of Monseigneur. He had been some few leagues behind Monseigneur, early in the afternoon. He had diminished the distance rapidly, but not so rapidly as to come up with Monseigneur on the road.
>
> (bk. 2, chap. 9)

The nephew of Monseigneur arrives and dines with his uncle. Their genteel conversation reveals a deadly turn of mind, particularly on the part of the Marquis, whose face

> was cruelly, craftily and closely compressed, while he stood looking quietly at his nephew, with his snuff-box in his hand.

Once again he touched him on the breast, as though his finger were the fine point of a small sword, with which, in delicate finesse, he ran him through the body.

(bk. 2, chap. 9)

However, Charles himself alludes to his uncle's death—something the Marquis is quick to comment on:

"This property and France are lost to me," said the nephew, sadly; "I renounce them."

"Are they both yours to renounce? France may be, but is the property? It is scarcely worth mentioning; but, is it yet?"

"I had no intention, in the words I used, to claim it yet. If it passed to me from you, to-morrow—"

"Which I have the vanity to hope is not probable."

(bk. 2, chap. 9)

But the Marquis, in his vanity, is mistaken. Before dawn, he will be "run through" in the very chambers where they speak, by the shadowy, gaunt figure who has moved in and out of his thoughts all day, trading places with his nephew.

The Marquis has desired the death of his nephew, and Charles, more covertly, has imagined the sudden death of his father's twin. There is the suggestion, but never the realization, of both filicide and patricide. But the exchange between the Marquis and his nephew is framed by the murder of a child and the murder of the Marquis himself. The former symbolizes the Marquis's murderous impulses toward his brother's child, as well as the cruelty of the French ruling classes toward their dependents, like the abuse witnessed by Doctor Manette eighteen years earlier. At the same time, the revenge that follows is both an actualization of Charles's revenge against his father's surrogate and a gesture that shows the French peasantry rising up to murder its rulers, as they will ultimately murder the father of their country in the revolutionary act of regicide. Dickens clarifies these connections when he describes the rumors that follow the capture of the Marquis's assassin:

"He is brought down into our country to be executed on the spot, and . . . he will very certainly be executed. They even whisper that because he has slain Monseigneur, and because Monseigneur was the father of his tenants—serfs—what you will—he will be executed as a parricide. . . . his right hand,

armed with the knife, will be burnt off before his face . . .
into wounds which will be made in his arms, his breast, and
his legs, there will be poured boiling oil, melted lead, hot
resin, wax, and sulphur; finally . . . he will be torn limb
from limb by four strong horses."

(bk. 2, chap. 15)

That Darnay should flee such a country is hardly surprising, but
the political reasons for flight are intensified by his personal desire to
avoid the retribution prophesied by his mother for the sins of his
fathers. And the futility of that flight becomes apparent with his return
to France after the Revolution. Darnay's fate is to be forced, against
his conscious desire, into a deadly struggle with his fathers: his own
father, his father's identical twin, his father-in-law. Although Darnay
and Manette learn to respect and love each other, their goodwill is
repeatedly subverted by events. Charles's marriage to Lucie nearly kills
Manette, and Manette's document in turn condemns Darnay to the
guillotine. The characters seem to be moved by something larger than
their individual desires, by the sins of a nation, which inevitably lead
only to more sin, to an orgy of murder and retribution. The political
meaning of these acts is intensified by a deep and persistent psychological theme, at times so perfectly merged with the political that one and
the same act may be construed as personal revenge, patricide, and
regicide.

If the murderer of Evrémonde symbolically enacts Darnay's violence and vengeance, then Sydney Carton enacts another side of Darnay's
character and pays for the hero's aggression. Carton's sacrifice is a
convenient, if implausible, device to free Charles from the Bastille; it is
also an attempt to solve an insoluble political dilemma. The revolutionaries justifiably overthrow their rulers, but their hatred leads to
excesses that turn despised oppressor into sympathetic victim. The sins
of the fathers are endlessly repeated, from generation to generation,
and Dickens's unrealistic solution creates a character who, Christ-like,
will sacrifice himself for the sins of all mankind. But Carton's transformation from guilty scoundrel to hero also indicates a deeper, psychological transformation. This paragon of irreverence, having mocked
and antagonized Mr. Lorry, now achieves a sudden closeness to the old
banker. He notices Lorry crying over Charles's plight:

"You are a good man and a true friend," said Carton,
in an altered voice. "Forgive me if I notice that you are

affected. I could not see my father weep, and sit by, careless. And I could not respect your sorrow more, if you were my father. You are free from that misfortune, however."

(bk. 3, chap. 9)

For the first time in his knowledge of Carton, Lorry sees a "true feeling and respect"; once he decides to sacrifice himself, Carton becomes something like an ideal son and rediscovers his father in Lorry. Sydney then thinks back to his youth, and his dead father:

> Long ago, when he had been famous among his earliest competitors as a youth of great promise, he had followed his father to the grave. His mother had died, years before. These solemn words, which had been read at his father's grave, arose in his mind as he went down the dark streets, among the heavy shadows, with the moon and the clouds sailing on high above him. "I am the resurrection and the life, saith the Lord: he that believeth in me, though he were dead, yet shall he live: and whosoever liveth and believeth in me, shall never die."
>
> (bk. 3, chap. 9)

These words dominate Carton's subsequent feelings. He transforms his life by internalizing his father's image, using Lorry as a surrogate: his earlier aimlessness dissolves and a new mission identifies him with the most famous—and self-sacrificing—of sons. Carton begins to achieve a sense of historical and personal identity, and the novel ends with Carton reborn through his namesakes, Lucie's son and grandson. And with Carton's newfound strength and purpose, Darnay becomes "like a young child in [Carton's] hands." Unconscious, Darnay is delivered to old Manette and Lucie and carried out of France like a sleeping baby (bk. 3, chap. 8). This sequence suggests that, as the hero's double internalizes paternal authority and willingly sacrifices himself to it, the innocent hero may be reborn.

The British world of business offers a different, more pragmatic solution to father-son struggles. Samuel Smiles, a widely read apostle for the self-made man, speaks for a common British chauvinism when he contrasts England and France:

> [The English system] best forms the social being, and builds up the life of the individual, whilst at the same time it perpetuates the traditional life of the nation . . . thus we

come to exhibit what has so long been the marvel of
foreigners—a healthy activity of individual freedom, and yet
a collective obedience to established authority—the unfet-
tered energetic action of persons, together with the uniform
subjection of all to the national code of Duty.

(*Self-Help*)

This description integrates independent action and submission to authority. Because Dickens's France prevents such integration, unre-
strained selfishness and anarchy tear the country apart. Although England
has both unruly mobs and abundant selfishness, the British control the
central conflict between sons and fathers, independence and authority.
In a land of opportunity the individual submits himself to a generalized
authority, which he then internalizes—at least according to Smiles and
most other Victorians. The virtues of "promptitude," "energy," "tact,"
"integrity," "perseverance"—the whole list of ingredients in Smiles's
recipe for success in business—involve the same psychological dynamic: turn external tyranny into internal censorship and control.
Self-Help opposes external help. Patronage, money, support in any
form inhibit imitating one's business "fathers" and, by struggle and
hard work, repeating their success. Government itself is internalized:
"It may be of comparatively little consequence how a man is governed
from without, whilst everything depends upon how he governs himself from within. The greatest slave is not he who is ruled by a despot
. . . but he who is the thrall of his own moral ignorance, selfishness,
and vice" (Smiles). The description fits Carton perfectly, at least until
his conversion. Carton demonstrates his moral degeneration by willingly playing jackal to Stryver's pompous lion. Their relationship in
turn demonstrates the Victorian businessman's divided personality: he
hopes to rise in the world but he must never become a "striver,"
particularly in a field like law, where one must appear unruffled, cool,
above all a gentleman. Dickens's social insight is conveyed by caricature and specifically by a psychological division that embodies an
enforced social separation, not unlike the two sides to Wemmick in
Great Expectations.

Smiles's ideal is to rise gracefully, working hard but never seem-
ing to toil or manipulate. He tells the story of an architect who, in
spite of extensive education and training abroad, was forced to start
humbly: "He determined to begin anywhere, provided he could be
employed. . . . he had the good sense not to be above his trade, and he

had the resolution to work his way upward . . . he persevered until he advanced by degrees to more remunerative branches of employment. Charles Darnay does the same:

> With great perseverance and untiring industry, he prospered.
>
> In London, he had expected neither to walk on pavements of gold, nor to lie on beds of roses: if he had had any such exalted expectation, he would not have prospered. He had expected labour, and he found it, and did it, and made the best of it. In this, his prosperity consisted.
>
> (bk. 2, chap. 10)

For Carton, however, such qualities are only "a mirage of honourable ambition, self-denial, and perseverance" (bk. 2, chap. 5). He denies his own ambition and projects it onto the gross reality of Stryver.

The two cities of Dickens's *Tale* embody two very different public expressions of father-son conflict. In England, particularly in the world of business, repression is internalized: it becomes a psychological act rather than a political one. As public repression is diminished, internal aggression is brought under control, and the generation in power transmits its own authority—its own image—to those who follow. In France, political repression is much stronger, as is the political retaliation of the oppressed. Dickens distorted the reality of the French Revolution to fit precisely into this liberal vision of the causes of revolution (and the need for a prophylactic reform), exaggerating the brutality and repression of the ancien régime and reducing the uprising itself to a nightmare of populist, radical reaction. Dickens's historical distortion clearly states the prevailing British liberal attitudes toward political repression and reform, toward the value of business and free enterprise, and, implicitly, toward the frequent, and frequently unconscious, struggle between fathers and sons throughout the century.

Jarvis Lorry is the ideal businessman. Business may be Lorry's defense against feeling, as he hints in his warning to Lucie that "all the relations I hold with my fellow-creatures are mere business relations" (bk. 1, chap. 4); but his thorough identification with his employer, Tellson's, endows them with a mercantile nobility. Fearing that Tellson's customers would be compromised by the seizure or destruction of documents—"for who can say that Paris is not set afire to-day, or sacked to-morrow"—he decides that he alone can protect their interests. His age and personal safety are not at issue: "Shall I hang back, when Tellson's knows this and says this—Tellson's, whose bread I have eaten these sixty years—because I am a little stiff about the joints? Why, I am a boy, sir, to half a dozen old codgers here!" (bk. 2, chap. 24). Lorry's language demonstrates not only his chivalry but also his clear filial relation toward his "House," which feeds him; his identification with Tellson's also gives him strength and, significantly, youth. At several points in this scene Darnay repeats his admiration for Lorry's "gallantry and youthfulness."

Elsewhere in the novel, Dickens describes the peculiar business education provided by Tellson's:

> When they took a young man into Tellson's London house, they hid him somewhere till he was old. They kept him in a dark place, like a cheese, until he had the full Tellson flavour and blue-mould upon him. Then only was he permitted to be seen, spectacularly poring over large books, and casting his breeches and gaiters into the general weight of the establishment.
>
> (bk. 2, chap. 1)

Although the obvious satire here may temper Lorry's heroism, it is, for Dickens, comparatively gentle, and its humor softens the antagonism between the old and the young. Dickens is certainly not flattering in his appraisal of Tellson's—"very small, very dark, very ugly, very incommodious" (bk. 2, chap. 1)—but his criticism of this dangerously antiquated operation is checked by a humorous acceptance, a feeling that, old-fashioned as it is, it produces good men, trust, honor. Smiles, too, stresses the heroism of banking:

> Trade tries character perhaps more severely than any other pursuit in life. It puts to the severest tests honesty, self-denial, justice, and truthfulness; and men of business who pass through such trials unstained are perhaps worthy of as great honour as soldiers who prove their courage amidst the fire and perils of battle . . . reflect but for a moment on the vast amount of wealth daily entrusted even to subordinate persons . . . and note how comparatively few are the breaches of trust which occur amidst all this temptation. . . . the system of Credit, which is mainly based upon the principle of honour, would be surprising if it were not so much a matter of ordinary practice in business transactions. . . . the

implicit trust with which merchants are accustomed to con-
fide in distant agents . . . often consigning vast wealth to
persons, recommended only by their character . . . is probably the finest act of homage which men can render to one
another.

Through a characteristic reference to parents and children, Dickens equates Tellson's with England: "Any one of [the] partners would
have disinherited his son on the question of rebuilding Tellson's. In
this respect the House was much on a par with the Country" (bk. 2,
chap. 1). Compare this mild satire with the savagery of Dickens's
attack on other bureaucratic strongholds, like the Circumlocution Office of *Little Dorrit*. The very name "Tell son" enjoins the paternalistic
institution to reveal to its dependents the secrets of the House, although it takes a ridiculously long time to do so. Imparting secrets to a
son resolves not only generational conflict but also the problem of
spying. Wait long enough, the "sons" are implicitly advised, make the
interests of the House *your* interests, internalize the father's authority,
and all things will become known.

A Tale of Two Cities has been consistently criticized for what
Dickens himself called its "want of humour." John Gross writes:

Above all, the book is notoriously deficient in humour. One
falls—or flops—back hopefully on the Crunchers, but to
small avail. True, the comic element parodies the serious
action: Jerry, like his master, is a "Resurrection-Man," but
on the only occasion that we see him rifling a grave it turns
out to be empty, while his son's panic-stricken flight with
an imaginary coffin in full pursuit is nightmarish rather than
funny.

Young Jerry's experience occurs in the chapter entitled "The Honest
Tradesman" (bk. 2, chap. 14), and its comedy, which is indeed closer
to nightmare, extends the "serious action" of the novel more thoroughly than Gross allows: "The Honest Tradesman" combines national, commercial, and generational conflict.

Above all else, Young Jerry is "impelled by a laudable ambition to
study the art and mystery of his father's honest calling" (bk. 2, chap.
14). We see this particular scene through the boy's own close-set,
staring eyes, and the landscape reflects Jerry's spying, his desire to see
into the mystery of his father's nocturnal expeditions: lamps "wink,"

while the gravestones and the church tower spy in turn on the prying men and the peeping child. Jerry witnesses a peculiar form of "fishing":

> They fished with a spade, at first. Presently the honoured parent appeared to be adjusting some instrument like a great corkscrew. Whatever tools they worked with, they worked hard, until the awful striking of the church clock so terrified Young Jerry, that he made off, with his hair as stiff as his father's.
>
> (bk. 2, chap. 14)

The language amuses us in part because it is sexually suggestive, with its "great corkscrew" and the hair that stands up and stiffens. But such language also comically expresses Young Jerry's ambition to grow up and become his father. His desire to find out what his father does and to emulate him inverts the novel's dominant struggle: the identical appearance of the Crunchers defines their essential unity. Resemblance—sinister in the Evrémonde twins and dramatic and theatrical between Carton and Darnay—is here the comic assertion of a common identity. Jerry Jr. is a perfect replica of his parents, and a perfect parody of the conservative ideal. At first annoyed by his child's curiosity, Jerry Sr. finally responds with favor because he realizes that this family succession offers no threat at all; the son will forfeit his own identity to take on his father's: "There's hopes wot that boy will yet be a blessing to you," Jerry Sr. says to himself, "and a recompense to you for his mother!" (bk. 2, chap. 14).

The father's pursuit of an "honest trade" has more than a mercantile meaning for his son, as Dickens's ambiguous language suggests throughout this chapter:

> There was a screwing and complaining sound down below, and their bent figures were stained, as if by a weight. By slow degrees the weight broke away the earth upon it, and came to the surface. Young Jerry very well knew what it would be; but, when he saw it, and saw his honoured parent about to wrench it open, he was so frightened, being new to the sight, that he made off again, and never stopped until he had run a mile or more.
>
> (bk. 2, chap. 14)

The following morning, Jerry wakes up to see his father beating his mother on their bed for something that had gone wrong during the night, something attributed to her praying or "flopping tricks"—a term, like "Resurrection-Man," that parodies both religion and sex. Jerry's surname indicates his feeling for his wife, his desire to crunch her, and that mixed demonstration of sexuality and violence characterizes his language. "You have no more nat'ral sense of duty," he tells her, "than the bed of this here Thames river has of a pile, and similarly it must be knocked into you" (bk. 2, chap. 14).

Jerry's language, like his mysterious nocturnal affairs, parodies the sexual violence of the Evrémondes' rape described by Doctor Manette. In one sense the comic episode may be read as another primal scene: a boy spies on his father's mysterious doings at night and later witnesses his father beating his mother on their bed; throughout, the language is both violent and implicitly sexual. At the same time, the comedy reproduces the combination of father-son conflict and social struggle present in Manette's story and traced throughout the novel. Yet because it approximates a primal scene so closely, the characteristic merging of violence and sexuality becomes here more grotesque than funny. Such language, like Jerry's generally ambiguous behavior, strains the text and limits its comic effectiveness. John Gross observes that the resurrection theme cannot justify what Jerry does; however, the resurrection theme is itself subordinate to the larger thematic struggle between sons and fathers. The structure of "The Honest Tradesman" reflects the structure of the *Tale*: it is at once psychological and social, suggesting both a child's vision of is parents' sexuality and the historical nightmare of the French Revolution. The comedy revises the novel's central conflicts and offers its own resolution. But that resolution cannot be sustained, and both the language and the setting of the comedy too strongly reveal the nightmare that informs it.

Dickens's familial and political revolutions are expressed by his varied use of splitting throughout the novel, so that the theme of the work becomes as well its characteristic mode of expression. From the title through the rhetorically balanced opening paragraphs, Dickens establishes the "twoness" of everything to follow: characters are twinned and doubled and paired; the setting is doubled; the women, as we shall see, are split; the historical perspective is divided between an eighteenth-century event and its nineteenth-century apprehension. "Splitting" thus describes a variety of stylistic devices, particularly related to character development and plot. But "splitting" also has two important psychoanalytic meanings: a splitting of the individual (specifically, the ego) and a splitting of the object. That is, an individual may deal with a specific problem, relationship, or trauma either by dividing himself or by dividing the problematic "other" (parent, loved one). Splitting is a fundamental mode of psychological defense and a key concept in the development of psychoanalytic theory. It originated in a description of schizophrenia and is now recognized as a central mechanism of multiple personality; but it may also be part of a normal adaptive strategy for coping with any intense relationship.

Dickens manipulates both emotional conflict and its solution by "splitting" in the technical, psychoanalytic sense: his characters distance their emotions from an immediate, and disturbing, reality (thus Lorry's remark to Lucie about his lack of feeling or Carton's apparent ability to separate himself from everything except the "higher" emotions at the close); he divides a single ego into two (Carton/Darnay); and he splits the "object," allowing one person (Charles's uncle) to bear the brunt of the hero's hatred or aggression toward Charles's father. Conversely, Dickens's use of doubles may suggest, not splitting, but reunifying something once divided or divisible: the comic identification of Jerry Jr. with his father or the larger movement between London and Paris, which connects seemingly disparate incidents and persons and ultimately unites the two plots. Even in the famous rhetoric of the opening, the balanced opposites suggest their own ultimate fusion. The use of splitting in a work this long is too varied and extensive to justify simple praise or blame—splitting is primarily a descriptive term—but it should clarify the understandably divided critical assessment of the novel.

Fitzjames Stephen had originally called the book's tone "thoroughly contemptible," while Dickens thought it could be the best story he had written. Sylvère Monod makes a more balanced appraisal, noting the special intensity of the revolutionary passages but finding the origins of that intensity in a "personal interest" that breaks down the proper distance between author and subject. Monod at times seems to withdraw his approval, but he is simply reflecting the work's contradictory quality: "Few would refuse to admit that the *Tale* is very much a contrived product," he has recently written, "[or] that the contrivance is usually superb." In addition to citing the lack of sustained comedy in the novel, critics have complained about the contrivance and sentimentality of Carton's role and about Dickens's oversimplification of a complex historical event. I have suggested that the failed comedy of the Crunchers derives, in part, from a failure to control, or sufficiently disguise, the primal-scene material implicit throughout the text. Dickens's historical oversimplification reflects, as we have seen, a merging of family and class struggles that was both characteristic and particularly problematic in the nineteenth century. Carton's role, both as a "double" to the hero and as a melodramatic scapegoat at the close, develops the dual conflicts of the novel; indeed, much of the sentimentality of Carton-as-Christ is derived from his conversion, via Lorry, into the good son and the good conservative. Carton's solution is that of any son—or class—that willingly accepts the pain or injustice inflicted upon it by parents or rulers, and such a solution is not particularly satisfying to most readers. In his peculiarly calm and heroic way, Carton stands for the ideals of conservative belief, in the family and the nation, but he finally assumes too many meanings and is required to connect too many threads of the novel. He suffers chronically from meaning too much in relation to too many other characters and themes and, like Manette's document, unites too many incidents; he becomes more strained as he becomes more important.

Other kinds of splitting in *A Tale of Two Cities* far more successfully project the text's central conflicts, precisely because they require no resolution. Dickens's caricature of the lion and the jackal, for example, exploits an inherent, unresolvable tension in his social subject. The division of labor between Carton and Stryver powerfully suggests not only Carton's divided self but the divided goals and morals of Victorian business. Divided imagery, like split objects, also contributes to the intense passages describing the Terror:

> False eyebrows and false moustaches were stuck upon them, and their hideous countenances were all bloody and sweaty, and all awry with howling, and all staring and glaring with beastly excitement and want of sleep. . . . men stripped to the waist, with the stain all over their limbs and bodies; men in all sorts of rags, with the stain upon those rags; men devilishly set off with spolls of women's lace and silk and ribbon, with the stain dyeing those trifles through and through. Hatchets, knives, bayonets, swords, all brought to be sharpened, were all red with it.
>
> (bk. 3, chap. 2)

The passage effectively combines images and emotions that the Victorians normally separated. In the revolutionary scenes the women are characteristically stronger and more savage than the men. Dickens further confuses sexual roles by connecting delicate and deadly images: "lace and silk and ribbons . . . Hatchets, knives, bayonets, swords." And these images in turn anticipate the hellish dance of the revolutionaries:

> They advanced, retreated, struck at one another's hands, clutched at one another's heads, spun round alone, caught one another and spun round in pairs, until many of them dropped. While those were down, the rest linked hand in hand, and all spun round together: then the ring broke, and in separate rings of two and four they turned and turned until they all stopped at once, began again, struck, clutched, and tore, and then reversed the spin, and all spun round another way. . . . No fight could have been half so terrible as this dance. It was so emphatically a fallen sport—a something, once innocent, delivered over to all devilry—a healthy pastime changed into a means of angering the blood, bewildering the senses, and steeling the heart. Such grace as was visible in it, made it the uglier, showing how warped and perverted all things good by nature were become. The maidenly bosom bared to this, the pretty almost-child's head thus distracted, the delicate foot mincing in this slouth of blood and dirt, were types of the disjointed time.
>   This was the Carmangole.
>
> (bk. 3, chap. 5)

Both passages sharply juxtapose opposites: murder and celebration, ritual and anarchy, violence and delicacy. The dance itself is vividly sexual, orgiastic in fact; and witnessing a perverse "sport" more awful than any fight, an innocence now delivered into hell, intensifies the terror of this scene.

A Tale of Two Cities reflects the Victorian repudiation of sexual or powerful women by contrasting the dull but idealized heroine and her more dangerous, sexual counterpart. Madame Defarge is an almost mythically frightening woman with male strength, but she has as well an animal-like beauty:

> [a] beauty . . . impart[s] to its possessor firmness and animosity. . . . a tigress. . . .
>   Such a heart Madame Defarge carried under her rough robe. Carelessly worn, it was a becoming robe enough, in a certain weird way, and her dark hair looked rich under her

coarse red cap. Lying hidden in her bosom, was a loaded pistol. Lying hidden at her waist, was a sharpened dagger. Thus accoutred, and walking with the confident tread of such a character, and with the supple freedom of a woman who had habitually walked in her girlhood, barefoot and bare-legged, on the brown sea-sand, Madame Defarge took her way along the streets.

(bk. 3, chap. 14)

Many subsequent versions of Madame Defarge, in film and in illustration, have made her a witch. The Harper and Row cover to *A Tale of Two Cities,* for example, shows a cadaverous old crone, gray-haired, hunched over her knitting, with wrinkles stitched across a tightened face. The original "Phiz" illustration, however, brings out Madame Defarge's beauty, her dark hair and her "supple freedom"; if we compare this with two later illustrations of Lucie, we realize that Madame Defarge is a strong, dark-haired version of the heroine. Characteristically, Dickens gives the Frenchwomen vitality, conveyed negatively as animality ("tigress"), and denies his heroine these qualities. The Frenchwomen infuse their vitality into the "fallen sport" of the Carmagnole, until they appear like "fallen women," inhabiting a world of violence and overt sexuality. For Madame Defarge's sister, aristocratic brutality extends even to violation. The clearest antecedent of Madame Defarge herself is her compatriot, Mademoiselle Hortense, from *Bleak House*. Hortense "would be handsome," laments Dickens, "but for a certain feline mouth. . . . she seems to go about like a very neat She-Wolf imperfectly tamed." She is both attractive and frightening, and her violence is expressed by sexuality. When Bucket tells Hortense that Mrs. Bucket has helped to trap her, Hortense replies, "tigress-like":

> "I would like to kiss her!" . . .
> "You'd bite her, I suspect," says Mr. Bucket.
> "I would!" making her eyes very large. "I would love to tear her, limb from limb."

Hortense virtually becomes Madame Defarge when she applies to Esther for service, and Esther finds that the "lowering energy" of the woman "seemed to bring visibly before me some woman from the streets of Paris in the reign of terror."

Lucie, by contrast, is the perfect Victorian female, the ideal home companion, a loving stereotype. She achieves blandness by playing *both* child and mother (and largely skipping anything in between), so that she is all things to all generations. Darnay acknowledges that Lucie's love for her father is "an affection so unusual, so touching . . . that it can have few parallels":

> "When she is clinging to you, the hands of baby, girl, and woman, all in one, are round your neck. . . . in loving you she sees and loves her mother at her own age, sees and loves you at my age, loves her mother brokenhearted, loves you through your dreadful trial and in your blessed restoration. I have known this, night and day, since I have known you in your home."
>
> Her father sat silent, with his face bent down.
>
> (bk. 2, chap. 10)

Most readers, unfortunately, do the same.

Dickens's violent and passionate Frenchwomen characterize not only the Carmagnole but virtually every set scene of the Revolution: "The men were terrible, in the bloody-minded anger with which they looked from windows, caught up what arms they had, and came pouring down into the streets; but, the women were a sight to chill the boldest" (bk. 2, chap. 22). While the rape of Madame Defarge's sister dramatizes the exploitation of personal "wealth," Madame Defarge turns beauty into power and violence, finally into terror. Her revenge is all the more awful because it reverses the sister's helplessness—or, more generally, the assumed passivity of Victorian women and of the lower classes. Madame Defarge is more implacable than her husband; her closest ally is a woman who personifies revenge; and the most murderous and frightening figure of all is "the figure of the sharp female called La Guillotine" (bk. 3, chap. 4). The Frenchwomen embody Dickens's political moral: the more violently you exploit and distort in one direction, the more violent and distorted will be the reaction. And Dickens frames his moral with the language of procreation and violation: "Sow the same seed of rapacious license and oppression over again, and it will surely yield the same fruit according to its kind" (bk. 3, chap. 15).

Throughout his career, Dickens split both his hero and the hero's loved ones, particularly in a setting of generational conflict. Monks, the villainous half-brother of Oliver Twist, and Uriah Heep and Steerforth in *David Copperfield* establish a pattern of the hero's guilt and expiation that would later define the essential relationship between Carton and Darnay. In *Oliver Twist* there is also a simple parental choice—Brownlow or Fagin—that becomes far more complex in *David Copperfield,* when David, in his first marriage, seems to behave like his hated stepfather, Murdstone. Dickens makes a more complex use of split egos and split objects in *A Tale of Two Cities,* although he handles splitting most successfully in the novel that immediately follows: *Great Expectations* extensively uses alter egos, and its action is built around Pip's developing relationship to his various fathers—Joe, Jaggers, Magwitch. By returning to the first-person narrative of *David Copperfield,* Dickens united—internalized—the conflicts that were externalized in *A Tale of Two Cities* and never satisfactorily reunited at its close. Pip is both Darnay and Carton, he is both heroic and guilty, and he even experiences the complex conflicts of the Victorian world of business, as described here in *A Tale of Two Cities.*

Edgar Johnson has written that "*A Tale of Two Cities* has been hailed as the best of Dickens's books and damned as the worst. It is neither, but it is certainly in some ways the least characteristic." This essay tries to show, on the contrary, that in *A Tale of Two Cities* Dickens is concerned with two connected themes that preoccupied him throughout his career: the generational and political conflicts he repeatedly expressed through the technique of splitting. However, because that technique is used so pervasively in *A Tale of Two Cities,* it makes the novel seem uncharacteristically concentrated in style and, at times, uncharacteristically strained or humorless. The novel's particular combination of individual psychology and broad social concerns thus accounts for its unique qualities, its intensity, and its failures. *A Tale of Two Cities* dramatizes two dominant conflicts of the Victorian age—and of our own.

The Purity of Violence:
A Tale of Two Cities

John Kucich

After years of neglect, *A Tale of Two Cities* has probably become the most vigorously defended of Dickens's works. Recently, we have had numerous apologies for the novel that have uncovered its psychological complexities, its historical relevance, and the subtleties of its style with remarkable acuity. All of these critiques reveal that Dickens's novel is more sophisticated and more rewarding than has often been recognized. And yet, all of them seem to conclude that the novel ultimately fails in an important way: it adumbrates complex problems that escape the limited range of its "solution"—Sydney Carton's Christlike martyrdom—which remains artificial, inadequate, and even embarrassing. This constant dissatisfaction with the ending implies that the fundamental problem for readers of *A Tale of Two Cities* is not the novel's general framework of ideas; the more serious problem is the novel's inability to provide an ethical or an analytical resolution—a useful resolution—to the social and psychological problems it announces, and its apparent willingness to submerge those problems in the stagey, emotionally-charged but intellectually vapid crescendoes of melodrama. In other words, what we have here is a problem with narrative mode: it is the form of the novel that troubles modern readers, that frustrates expectations generated by the rest of the novel.

At the risk of bringing us full circle back to the grounds of early complaints against *A Tale of Two Cities,* I suggest that the serious uses of melodrama in the novel must be stressed if we are to understand its aesthetic wholeness. Spawned by Wilkie Collins's melodrama *The Fro-*

From *Dickens Studies Annual* 8 (1980). © 1980 by AMS Press, Inc.

zen Deep, Dickens's novel has the play's emotional excessiveness at its very core, and any attempt to clarify the novel's thematic structure must therefore take up the challenge of that excessiveness. Recent studies have shown that debating melodrama's legitimacy as a literary mode is less profitable than articulating the ends that melodrama tries to achieve, if only in the interest of broadening our notions about the possible—and impossible—goals of narrative structure. In the case of *A Tale of Two Cities,* Dickens's novelistic goals depend heavily upon his melodramatic plot. In my view, the non-rational impulses behind melodrama develop a crucial authorial intention: Dickens's novel consistently works toward an escape from the realm of the analytical, the ethical, and the useable altogether. Instead, the novel investigates and defends desires for irrational extremity that it satisfies finally in Carton's chaste suicide. Dickens's attitude toward the role of emotional excess in human life, which is elaborately defined as the work unfolds, logically carries the novel away from orderly, intellectually apprehendable resolutions toward a more dynamic goal: the staging of acceptable—as opposed to cruel—violence.

A *Tale of Two Cities* is not a revolutionary novel, in the sense that it advocates political and social revolt, but it does dramatize a pressing, fundamental human need for liberating change of the most extreme kind. Dickens's novel is an enactment of human needs for an extreme release from many different kinds of confinement, and, in these terms, the novel's crucial development is a subtle change in the way violence can be valued as a vehicle for such release. That is to say, general needs for a victory over repression, which the novel embodies as a desire for violence, are purified as they are moved from the social context of the novel into the personal one: the revolutionaries' problematical desires for freedom are translated into acceptable terms by the good characters in their own struggles for freedom, and they are focused finally in the "pure" self-violence of Sydney Carton, which liberates him from self-hatred. In an abstract sense, what this means finally is that the novel's symbolic logic affirms Carton's initial tendencies toward an internal kind of violence—his dissipation—under the guise of his later, moral "conversion." This assertion, of course, presents numerous difficulties, not the least of which is the problematical relationship between physical self-destruction and psychological liberation. But by reexamining Dickens's attitude toward excess and violence throughout the novel, we can begin to see why Carton's fate is unavoidable.

A non-specific, primary desire for a radical release from limits dominates the very texture of Dickens's novel. The famous opening paragraphs of the novel launch this movement toward release, articulating frustrated desires for extremity by way of parodying the desire of the historical imagination to erupt beyond the limits of conventional significance. Mixing the historian's typical desire to proclaim the extremity of his own elected period with undermining hints of the fundamental "sameness" of all ages, Dickens's much-quoted, much-sentimentalized opening catalogues the extremes of 1775 in a series of superlatives that cancel each other out: "It was the best of times, it was the worst of times, it was the age of wisdom, it was the age of foolishness, it was the epoch of belief, it was the epoch of incredulity . . ." (bk. 1, chap. 1). Despite themselves, these terms fail to produce a difference in meaning; instead, each term merely tends to produce its opposite, and to be bounded by it. In this way, the opening catalogue of extremes comments more on the needs of the historical imagination—and on those of the novelist—than on the actual tenor of any particular age. It emphasizes desires for extremity at the same time that it frustrates them. As he levels extremes, the narrator even claims that his own chosen epoch is not actually different from the present one—giving greater emphasis to his debunking satire—but that "in short, the period was so far like the present period, that some of its noisiest authorities insisted on its being received, for good or for evil, in the superlative degree of comparison only." Far from being extreme, the age is actually in the grip of a repetitive sameness in its very desire to be excessive, a desire which is trapped in conventional, competitive self-aggrandizements. And, on the level of political reality, the weighty repetition of desires for extremity is undisguised: "In both countries it was clearer than crystal to the lords of the State preserves of loaves and fishes, that things in general were settled for ever." Covertly, the belief that some kind of extremity has actually been reached becomes only the basis for dominance, as well as for repetition.

The pathetic desire for extremity within history introduces more successful desires for upheaval on the part of characters. In the beginning, for example, Sydney Carton's dissipation is presented as the result of a metaphysical crisis over limitations, and not as the vulgarity of the idle bum: Carton feels imprisoned by the banality of economic survival. Referring to himself as a "drudge," Carton, through his indifferently valued but very real skills and through his ostentatious rejection of preferment, deliberately affronts the acquisitive business world of Stryver. With sardonic pride, Carton flaunts his lack of

economic sense: "Bless you, *I* have no business" (bk. 2, chap. 4), he
tells Lorry. In keeping with this violation of the code of self-interest,
Carton had always instinctively done work for others rather than for
himself in school; and, professionally, he does all his work so that
Stryver, and not himself, may claim the credit and prosper. Carton's
utter intellectual competence to lead a successful, if ordinary, life gives
point to his rejection of self-concern, and defines it as a choice, however unconscious he may be of his own motives and however much
such a choice is painful, bringing along with it the anonymity of
self-abandonment. And, if Stryver and Lorry are examples of what
success means, then Carton's comparative genuiness—his freedom from
the rigidities of both aggression and repression—depends on his refusal
to value worldly success. It is interesting to note, too, that Jerry
Cruncher later stresses the unreality of the business world by claiming
that much normal business represses the final reality represented by
death; defending his graverobbing to Lorry, Cruncher observes: "There
might be medical doctors at the present hour, a picking up their
guineas where a honest tradesman don't pick up his fardens. . . . Then
wot with undertakers, and wot with parish clerks, and wot with
sextons, and wot with private watchmen (all awaricious and all in it), a
man wouldn't get much by it, even if it was so" (bk. 3, chap. 9). In the
context of the novel's sense that the business world is artificial, and
that it actively conceals the profounder reality of death, Carton's dissipation is a rejection of the world of petty survival on the broadest of
philosophical grounds: he tells Darnay simply that he wants to leave
"this terrestrial scheme" (bk. 2, chap. 4).

Despite the disapproval of other characters, the reader may find
Carton's carelessness and his reckless honesty refreshing. Carton's
dissipation is somehow "pure" precisely because it is free of self-
interest. From the very beginning, Dickens forces the reader to dis-
criminate between the popular judgment about Carton's degeneracy
and the possibility of his having hidden merits, often by putting his
condemnations of Carton into the wrong mouths. After all, it is the
ugly mob, feasting like flies on Darnay's trail, that finds Carton's
appearance disreputable, and it is Jerry Cruncher, after his vulgarity
has been established, who observes: "I'd hold half a guinea that *he*
don't get no law work to do. Don't look like the sort of one to get
any, do he?" (bk. 2, chap. 3). But Carton's superiority to the crowd
very soon emerges through his intensified powers of perception: "Yet,
this Mr. Carton took in more of the details of the scene than he

appeared to take in; for now, when Miss Manette's head dropped upon her father's breast, he was the first to see it, and to say audibly: 'Officer! look to that young lady. Help the gentleman to take her out. Don't you see she will fall!' " The mark of Carton's genius is this very ability to penetrate to the most important, the most essential levels—to see beyond the limited vision of others, or to say what others dare not say. In other words, Carton appeals to us through his freedom from convention and from constraint. Thus, his success at Darnay's trial is a single, bold, imaginative stroke, one that Stryver calls "a rare point" (bk. 2, chap. 5). His facility for "extracting the essence from a heap of statements" shows to advantage against Stryver's plodding determination, and his frankness shines out against Mr. Lorry's restraint—at Lorry's expense, Carton observes: "If you knew what a conflict goes on in the business mind, when the business mind is divided between good-natured impulse and business appearances, you would be amused, Mr. Darnay" (bk. 2, chap. 4). Lorry's exasperated reply defines the difference between himself and Carton explicitly: "Business is a very good thing, and a very respectable thing. And, sir, if business imposes its restraints and its silences and impediments, Mr. Darnay as a young gentleman of generosity knows how to make allowance for that circumstance." But to confirm the imposing dimensions of Carton's position, the narrator tells us that Lorry was "perhaps a little angry with himself, as well as with the barrister." In contrast, then, to the other good characters, whose lives are ruled by restraints of one kind or another, and despite our sense that we must disapprove of him, Carton stands out as the most vividly authentic character in the novel. Even in the love plot, Carton confides in Lucie more honestly than the others: Darnay conceals from Lucie his intended trip to France, and Manette tries to conceal from her his instinctual jealousy of Darnay. In the reader's eyes, Carton momentarily has a more intimate relationship with Lucie than either Darnay or Manette, for the reader sees Carton "open his heart" to her in the pivotal confession scene, the only scene in which a man expresses himself passionately to Lucie.

More importantly, perhaps, Carton's desire to release himself from constraints in dissipation, however much it is treated with repugnance by the good characters, is in fact not so far removed from their own desires. Darnay, who flees his own terrestrial scheme—France—is opposed to his uncle the Marquis in much the same way that Carton is opposed to Stryver (Stryver and the Marquis are linked later in the novel, when the lawyer gathers among the disinherited

French aristocracy at Tellson's and joins in their contempt for the French rebels and for the anonymous son of the Marquis). From the perspective of French aristocratic values, Darnay's teaching school is an unmentionable degradation, one that is essentially as demeaning as Carton's English unprofessionalism. And Darnay is eventually punished for this desertion of France, a punishment that implies allegorically—since it is difficult for us to understand how running from a French inheritance could be a crime—that there is some kind of moral transgression implicit in *any* release from normal human bonds. For Dr. Manette, too, release from prison is figured as a release from restrictive labor, which is represented by his obsessive shoe-making. His return home is emphasized imagistically as a release from the conservative claims of survival and self-interest largely because it frees him from the evasive narrowness of mind represented by his prison work-world. Though no longer functional, this work-world is an image of Dr. Manette's repression—his willingness to put on blinders and merely to endure, like all oblivious workmen. In its rigidly economic resonance, Manette's cobbling echoes Lorry's business-imposed restraint. However, the shadowy, disquieting destruction of Manette's work bench by Lorry and Miss Pross points to the guilt that inheres in the structure of such release: their destructive act is oddly congruent with the revolutionary destruction of the French mob. Darnay and Manette, like Sydney Carton, sin against an obscure moral law when they seek release from their respective imprisonments, no matter how much their freedom is approved by the reader.

Our ambivalent attitude toward Carton, then, is only an index of the generally problematic nature of almost any violated limits. By being political, generational, sexual, and vaguely misanthropic, desires for release in this novel acquire a kind of generality that transcends their local manifestations: such desires seem fundamentally human, while, at the same time, they seem ultimately threatening. The novel makes clear that while a desire for the destruction of psychological and social limitations may be profoundly human, it is always related to a desire for the destruction of restrictive personal identity in violence and in death.

It is worth noting at this point, as a way to approach the complex relationship between release from restrictions and death, that the confluence of desires for violent release with the potential transgression implied by such release dominates the background action. On the one hand, in the initial stages of the revolution in France, it is difficult not to sympathize with the laboring class's pursuit of freedom through violence. Occasionally, Dickens dwells on the mob's achievement of "human fellowship" through their uprising, and stresses the sympathetic unity of the oppressed people: "Not before dark night did the men and women come back to the children, wailing and breadless. Then, the miserable bakers' shops were beset by long files of them, patiently waiting to buy bad bread; and while they waited with stomachs faint and empty, they beguiled the time by embracing one another on the triumphs of the day, and achieving them again in gossip. Gradually, those strings of ragged people shortened and frayed away; and then poor lights began to shine in high windows, and slender fires were made in the streets, at which neighbours cooked in common, afterwards supping at their doors" (bk. 2, chap. 22). Then, too, the bursting wine cask scene, which mingles the sympathetic energy of a well-deserved holiday with ominous hints about the ultimate form of excessive "holiday" energy—the desire for blood, a word that someone writes into the wall in wine—also has the effect of linking the mob's exuberant expenditure of energy with Carton's drunkenness, as does the code name of the insurgents, the Jacques, link them with Carton and his sobriquet: the Jackal. And at this point early in the novel, both forms of energy—Carton's sottishness and the mob's— seem harmless and infinitely preferable to the alternative world of work. Like Carton's, too, the insurgents' drives for extremity have a metaphysical cast—though they do not consciously articulate it—in their collective willingness to risk life for something more valuable even than life: undefined, limitless freedom. The excessiveness of this risk of life, the way in which it breaks the mob loose from the repressive world of work, accounts for the ensuing eroticism—the mob's discovery that outside of the limits of self-concern is an idyllic world of plentitude and union: "Fathers and mothers who had had their full share in the worst of the day, played gently with their meagre children; and loves, with such a world around them and before them, loved and hoped" (bk. 2, chap. 22). Something of this plentitude of sexual arousal is also conveyed by the "Carmagnole," the dance of the rebels, which combines excessive violence with a polymorphous, eroticized fellow-feeling: "Men and women danced together, women danced together, men danced together, as hazard had brought them together. At first, they were a mere storm of coarse red caps and coarse woollen rags; but, as they filled the place, and stopped to dance about Lucie, some ghastly apparition of a dance-figure gone raving mad arose among them. They advanced, retreated, struck at one another's hands, clutched at one another's heads, spun round alone, caught one another and spun round in pairs, until many of them dropped" (bk. 2, chap. 5).

On the other hand, of course, the meaning of rebellion in France soon sours. Our reaction to the "Carmagnole" cannot be the same as our reaction to the crowd that dammed up flowing wine in the cobblestones. The scenes of violence are carefully built up to repel us gradually, and it is difficult to specify at what particular point we lose sympathy with the rebels. But it soon becomes clear that the mob's struggle for justice is totally outstripped by their brute satisfaction in the violence of dominance. Hence, although the mob's struggle has its roots in oppression and therefore takes our sympathy, the novel jolts us into a recognition of the form taken by the mob's desire for liberation—its inevitable tendency to congeal in cruelty, and to project what was once a "pure," disinterested violence outward against others.

The psychological dynamic here is specified by Hegel's Master-Slave dialectic: the Master is he who is most willing to give up his life for a greater, intangible good—a transcendent good not restricted by the economic taint of mere worldly survival. The Slave, then, is he who opts for survival rather than risking his life in a fight with the Master. In Hegel's dialectic, however, if the Master proves his greater willingness to face violent death and then survives because of the Slave's capitulation, this proved capacity for totalizing violence becomes the emblem and the instrument of his successful domination. The Master thus becomes trapped in petty factionalism when he seeks to make his transcendent liberation—proven through his willingness to die violently—endure in the form of the Slave's recognition of that transcendent violence. Consequently, there are two possible ways in which violence may be exercized: first, as a spontaneous release from slavishness through self-regardless violence—which, in temporal terms, is "pure" but also "meaningless" because it is not designed to be profitable; second, as a calculated retreat from self-abandonment toward the use of violence against others in an attempt to make one's transcendent liberation endure in the world. In terms of Dickens's novel, any desire for extremity that stops short of self-annihilation becomes impure by being implicated in the temporal arena of rivalry: most obviously, the mob projects violence outwards to preserve itself while affirming its claim to the righteousness and the transcendence implied by its willingness to confront death.

In *A Tale of Two Cities,* Hegel's two dialectical forms of violence are personified and set at war with each other. The purity of self-violence clearly belongs at first to the lower classes, who "held life as of no account, and were demented with a passionate readiness to sacrifice it" (bk. 2, chap. 21). Thus, the concrete effects of the revolutionaries' violence as an annihilation of their humanity—and, therefore, a violation of their human limitations—are actualized before us: we witness the transformation of rational figures like the Defarge couple into maddened beasts during the storming of the Bastille. Furthermore, to emphasize the "unnatural" and "non-human" element in the revolutionaries' passion, Dickens made their spokesperson a woman, since, in Dickens's world, the supreme disruption of normal expectations about human nature is an absence of tenderness in women. In the Parisian violence, even La Guillotine is female. And to heighten this effect, Madame Defarge's knitting in service of violence is set in sharp contrast to Lucie Manette's "golden thread" of pacification and harmony, as well as to the "domestic arts" that Lucie had learned in Madame Defarge's France. Most importantly, this yearning for the pure release of self-violence is identified as the ultimate form of desire for freedom through the good characters: Darnay, on his last night in prison, becomes fascinated with the guillotine—he has "a strange besetting desire to know what to do when the time came; a desire gigantically disproportionate to the few swift moments to which it referred; a wondering that was more like the wondering of some other spirit within his, than his own" (bk. 3, chap. 3). At one point, too, the narrator isolates the mob's fascination with the pure release of violent death, and makes of it a common human desire: "a species of fervour or intoxication, known, without doubt, to have led some persons to brave the guillotine unnecessarily, and to die by it, was not mere boastfulness, but a wild infection of the wildly shaken public mind. In seasons of pestilence, some of us will have a secret attraction to the disease—a terrible passing inclination to die of it. And all of us have like wonders hidden in our breasts, only needing circumstances to evoke them" (bk. 3, chap. 6). Thoughts like this lend a new resonance to the chapter title "Drawn to the Loadstone Rock," a chapter in which Darnay decides—for seemingly rational reasons, though he does refuse to discuss them with anyone who might restrain him—to go back to France, and help stress the novel's movement toward some kind of willed self-destruction.

The liberating intentions behind the lower classes' violence, however, are only a response to the repressive image of non-human freedom and "represented" violence that define the power of the class of Monseigneur. Instead of being defined through overt acts of violence, life among the upper classes revolves around static representations of their non-humanity—emblems of their willingness to violate human limits. The Marquis's own non-humanity marks itself in his freedom from emotion—the narrator at one point describes his appearance as being "a fine mask" (bk. 2, chap. 9), and his face is compared to the stone faces of his gargoyles. In his conversation with Charles, he annihilates feeling through the codified formality of manners: "the uncle made a graceful gesture of protest, which was so clearly a slight form of good breeding that it was not reassuring" (bk. 2, chap. 9). Generally, the hallmark of status among the Marquis's class is this "leprosy of unreality" (bk. 2, chap. 7). The Fancy Ball, for example, is full of "Unbelieving Philosophers," who construct elaborately meaning-less verbal structures, and "Unbelieving Chemists," who have their eyes on alchemy—both are in pursuit of the unnatural, through words or through metals. Good breeding itself "was at that remarkable time—and has been since—to be known by its fruits of indifference to every natural subject of human interest." Once again, too, the contrast is clearest in the image of the female; among the women of the Marquis's society, their chief distinction is their escape from maternity: it was "hard to discover among the angels of that sphere one solitary wife, who, in her manners and appearance, owned to being a Mother. . . . Peasant women kept the unfashionable babies close, and brought them up, and charming grandmammas of sixty dressed and supped as at twenty."

There is violence among the Marquis's class, of course, but it is colder, and has a clear function as a representation: that is, their violence is merely an occasional symbol of the mastery of the rich, since it proves their right to waste lives if they choose to—the lives of the lower orders. When the Marquis asserts that running down chil-dren with his carriage is a right of his station, he takes no passionate satisfaction from the killing; he takes only a numbed confirmation of his status. Initially, when the rebels in *A Tale of Two Cities* kill, they kill in passion, while the rich kill as spectacle—as, for example, when the royal government executes the murderer of the Marquis and leaves him hanging forty feet in the air. The Marquis expresses this functionality of violence explicitly; when Charles complains that his family is hated in France for their cruelty, the Marquis answers: "Let us hope so. . . . Detestation of the high is the involuntary homage of the low" (bk. 2, chap. 9).

The Hegelian horror of *A Tale of Two Cities* is this: at the point when the revolutionaries stop short of their own willingness to brave death and attempt to make their release permanent and meaningful in the form of a Republic, they trap themselves in the reified form of diverted violence—the petty, mechanical, and cruel contortions of human rivalry. We lost sympathy for the rebels when they lose sight of their limitless freedom—their "pure" release—and become trapped in their own revenge, thus imitating their oppressors. The very name of Madame Defarge's companion is "The Vengeance," and Madame Defarge undercuts herself through an ironic imitation: she dedicates herself to destroying the innocent Darnay family just as her own innocent family was destroyed. More disturbingly, for Madame Defarge, as for the rest of the revolutionaries, passionate revenge gives way to the invention of spurious rivalry, the murder of innocent victims. The purely mechanical quality of this imitative violence is underscored by the ominous note of historical destiny in this novel: the continuous references to things "running their courses" and the metaphors of echoing footsteps and approaching thunderstorms. In Dickens's novel, the "pure" wish for release always becomes tainted when it is diverted away from the self, and when the limits that are violated become the limits of others. The victory over repression on the part of the revolutionaries leads only to imprisonment in violent rivalry, just as Dr. Manette's liberation from imprisonment leads him directly into a rivalry with his own son-in-law, and just as Darnay's flight from France lands him squarely in a relationship of rivalry to Manette. In fact, the social and personal histories of *A Tale of Two Cities* converge on the theme of release that is trapped in rivalry: the novel dramatizes the failure even of Dickens's heroes to escape the structure of rivalry in their efforts to achieve release. In this novel, suppressing the rivalry inherent in release is not simply inadequate: it is elaborately examined as a strategy that fails.

Admittedly, against the background of class rivalry in France, it is at first a relief to find that the activity of the heroes is completely devoted to containing the potential rivalry inherent in their own relationships. Faced with the dangers latent in the relationships of Darnay to Carton and to Manette, the good characters try in every way to prevent rivalry from surfacing. Their virtue is entirely associated at first with repression, with their attempt to preserve relationships by denying the violence that is latent in them.

Lucie Manette is the primary reconciler and preserver—her "golden

thread" represents an attempt to weave together factions, and to inhibit the tendency of her men to displace each other. The other
characters co-operate universally with Lucie in her strategy of repression: Manette enjoins Darnay not to tell him the secret of Darnay's
own parentage; Darnay makes special efforts to conciliate Dr. Manette,
and to assure him that they are not competitors for Lucie's attentions;
Carton vows to Lucie that he will not envy Darnay, or pursue Lucie
herself in any romantic way; and Darnay promises Lucie that he will
hold no grudges against Carton. The minor character Miss Pross is
perhaps the most concise example of a thematics of suppression that
the novel seems at first to valorize: "Mr. Lorry knew Miss Pross to be
very jealous, but he also knew her by this time to be, beneath the
surface of her eccentricity, one of those unselfish creatures—found
only among women—who will, for pure love and admiration, bind
themselves willing slaves, to youth when they have lost it, to beauty
that they never had, to accomplishments that they were never fortunate enough to gain, to bright hopes that never shone upon their own
sombre lives" (bk. 2, chap. 6). It is interesting to note, too, that, as a
further emblem of the weight given to attempts to conserve, rather
than to violate or to rival, *A Tale of Two Cities* actually features a
businessman, Lorry, as one of its heroes—a rarity in Dickens. His
conservative role as banker even allows Lorry to travel safely between
the two cities: he is a kind of international reconciler. Moreover, his
functions in the plot are always rescue missions: his two dramatic
messages—"recalled to life" and "acquitted"—as well as his three
separate rescue operations in France are in sharp contrast to the operations of the only other business establishment in the novel, the Defarge's
wineshop, and to the aggressive business ethics expressed by Stryver.

However, while naked drives toward violence are repudiated
through the mob's factionalism, and, conversely, through Carton, whose
pure, non-competitive recklessness is merely ineffective, repression
taints the efforts of the good characters to suppress their own violence.
Their enforced restraint makes for an most bleak, numbed atmosphere
of good-will, instead of the generous flow of spirits necessary to
Dickens's vision of a closely knit, good society in his other novels. The
atmosphere of repression in the good characters' world is one reason
for the notorious want of humor in this novel, and it also echoes the
narrator's complaint, in the beginning of the novel, against the isolation of the individual within the narrow limits of personal identity: "A
wonderful fact to reflect upon, that every human creature is consti-

tuted to be that profound secret and mystery to every other. . . . Something of the awfulness, even of Death itself, is referable to this" (bk. 1, chap. 3). The "golden thread" foursome, though it obviously had Dickens's sympathy, participates in this gloomy fact of secrecy and repression. However sobering violence and rivalry may be, then, Dickens is ultimately on the side of change, and on the side of excess. The tone of the novel, as well as the awkward tension created by the proliferation of lovers for Lucie, speeds the novel toward some kind of rupture.

The inevitability of that rupture is signaled by a larger problem within the good characters' strategies of repression: in both of the crucial relationships among the good characters, inherent violence is only imperfectly suppressed, and finally emerges—even against the characters' wills—as rivalry. In the first conflict, Dr. Manette's voluntary suppression of his opposition to Darnay—which is both political, on account of the novel's germinal incident in France, and sexual, because they are locked in a relationship of natural, generational rivalry—is itself dangerous. Often, it sinks him back into the corrosive oblivion of work as he tries to screen out his jealousy. Lorry wonders "whether it is good for Dr. Manette to have that suppression always shut up within him" (bk. 2, chap.6). Even worse though, despite all his attempts to overcome it, Manette's involuntary rivalry with Darnay is mercilessly actualized by events. Manette's very attempts to save Darnay from the revolutionary tribunal are compromised by a dangerous, potential one-upmanship in his performance: "He was proud of his strength. 'You must not be weak, my darling,' he remonstrated; 'don't tremble so. I have saved him.' " (bk. 3, chap. 6). This one-upmanship is stressed by the Doctor's dependence on the rivalrous mob, which is devoted to Darnay's death. And, more significantly, the production of the document recounting the story of the Peasant Family realizes Manette's rivalry in a deadly way. Of course, Manette is passive in the confrontation: only in a moment of weakness and desperate yearning for freedom did he curse the aristocratic family that he never supposed he would see again; and the production of the fatal document is carried out here by others, against Manette's will. Still, on a symbolic level, the events enact an inevitable re-surfacing of rivalry as the temporal structure taken on by desires for liberation. Involuntarily, Manette is transformed from repressed victim to violent oppressor; he is identified with Madame Defarge and the rebels in their progress from one stage to the other.

In the second, more important rivalry, the one between Sydney Carton and Charles Darnay, the conditions of the rivalry are again involuntary: the two characters simply look alike, which stings Carton with a sense of his inferiority. Carton's metaphysical urges for violent release—like the desire of Manette for freedom, and like the desires of the lower class in this novel for liberation—is trapped in his envy of a rival, Darnay. Carton even selects his rival as the man who most completely displays a willingness to risk life, and who receives recognition for it: "Is it worth being tried for one's life," he says, "to be the object of such sympathy and compassion, Mr. Darnay?" (bk. 2, chap. 4). As a consequence, Carton's general bitterness about the limitations of his life focus themselves in this competition with Darnay for the clearest claim to violent self-expenditure and selflessness.

What makes the second relationship more interesting than the first is that Carton is finally able to satisfy his drive toward release in a morally legitimate way precisely through the structure of rivalry. Carton's "self-sacrifice," far from transcending structures of rivalry, actually operates within them. The will-to-power here is clear: Carton takes over Darnay's very handwriting and uses it to address an intimate message to Lucie, one that Darnay cannot understand or share; he refers to the unconscious Darnay as "me"; he envisions the surviving couple as "not more honoured and held sacred in each other's soul, than I was in the souls of both" (bk. 3, chap. 15); and he pictures Darnay's own son named after him, along with grandson also named after himself, who comes back to France solely for the purpose of hearing the Carton story. The crowning irony in Carton's violation of Darnay's identity and his claim to Lucie's admiration is that Carton is the one who projects the others' future in the last paragraphs of the novel, while both Manette and Darnay are lying in a coach, impotent and unconscious.

As Hegel teaches, until violence is directed back toward others, it is "meaningless" in temporal terms because it ends the life of self; similarly, Carton's early, non-competitive dissolution is meaningless—despite, or rather, because of the "purity" of the violence directed against himself. But Carton's death at the end of the novel does have a "meaning" on this side of death, and, like all such meanings, this one only expresses itself through the vehicle of rivalry; that is, Carton's sacrifice is meant to be compelling because it is superior to Darnay's, since Darnay's death would have been involuntary, and because it seems to make him "more worthy" of Lucie. Carton achieves a transcendent "meaning" only by demonstrating a greater willingness to face death. At the same time, however, Carton does not appropriate for himself any undesirable associations with mastery because he makes his self-expenditure complete. By losing his life, Carton annihilates self-interest. Moreover, besides the totality of his loss, Carton also nullifies any appropriation of recognition that he might conceivably desire by refusing to reveal his sacrifice to anyone while it is in preparation. Unlike Dr. Manette's ostentatious rescue of Darnay, Carton's proceeds in secret. He informs no one—not even Lorry—and he tells Lucie only in a note meant to be opened later, so that she would know that his life had not been "wantonly" thrown away. The awesome thing about Carton's death is just this: that he goes through it alone—he even dies under someone else's name (though recognition does come, innocuously, from a stranger on the scaffold, which implies that the reader's role in supplying necessary recognition that cannot come from within the world of the novel is crucial). And, ultimately, the violent aspect of Carton's "suicide" is redeemed through the preservation of Darnay and his family. Radical self-violence is balanced with meaning derived from its being put to temporal, conservative use. As an action, Carton's is the only violent release in the novel that can claim the readers' unqualified assent, since even actions like Dr. Manette's liberation from prison or Darnay's liberation from his English trial immediately cause new, unavoidable problems of rivalry.

Carton's death blends perfectly, almost ritualistically, the two irreconcilable human values of ultimate release and temporal survival, realizing through narrative an impossible wish. In this way, Carton's death violates our expectations about the limits of human action. Like Miss Pross, who changes the meaning of murder by losing her own hearing (as if in penance) and by saving the rest of the good characters when she kills Madame Defarge, Sydney Carton, by choosing death, changes the meaning of self-destruction: he carries out his earlier desires for dissipation free from the abyss of meaninglessness implied by self-annihilation—his death is actually sanctioned through its ability to preserve the Darnay family. Finally, for the reader, Carton helps to elevate our own fascination with violent extremity: rather than watching his death pruriently as the vulgar mob had watched Darnay's trial, we share in the condemned woman's religious awe.

If the conclusion of A Tale of Two Cities seems contrived, Dickens is well aware of at least one side of the contrivance: the rivalrous aspect of Carton's act is clearly articulated. Readers offended by the "simple-mindedness" of Carton's crucifixion can take solace in Dickens's awareness of this dimension to the act. At the same time, however, Dickens clearly intended the conclusion to move his readers unequivocally, as only the magnitude of death dramatized as a human desire could move them. What makes this ending melodramatic is not simply Carton's death, but his undiguised *desire* for death. We are well protected against this desire in our normal lives, and, as Peter Brooks points out [in *The Melodramatic Imagination*], one reason for critical embarrassment with the form of melodrama may very well be melodrama's refusal to censor itself. For this reason, whether the conclusion of *A Tale of Two Cities* moves or embarrasses us, the reason is the same: Dickens has presented us with an image of an explicitly desired violation of human limits, one that is presented as the only possible escape from the twin mechanisms of rivalry and repressed violence. In some of the later novels, Dickens attempts to make the liberation of self-violence possible through an intensified consciousness of death, chiefly through a kind of doubling within consciousness—the kind of doubling that enables Esther to "die" to Jarndyce but live for Woodcourt, and that enables Pip both to forget and to live for Estella. But, in *A Tale of Two Cities,* the synthesis of ultimate release and survival takes place only in the unstated relationship between Sydney Carton's death and the reader's awareness of that death's significance.

The Duplicity of Doubling in *A Tale of Two Cities*

Catherine Gallagher

For the past several years readers have been discovering that Victorian novels can be as ironically self-reflective as any novels. Now that they are expected to, Thackeray, Dickens, and George Eliot reveal the fictitiousness of their fictions, the constructed nature of their constructions, the wordiness of their worlds, as regularly as do Proust, Joyce, and Virginia Woolf. One of the primary techniques of Victorian self-reflectiveness that has lately attracted attention is the insertion into the novel of analogues for novelistic narration, analogues that expose the constructing operations of the narrator even as he or she pretends to be passively mirroring an objective reality. Several [recent] essays in [*Dickens Studies Annual*] call our attention to such analogues in *A Tale of Two Cities* and explain how, in themselves, they reveal the methods and intended effects of the narrative. This essay also addresses the topic of narrative analogues; however, it investigates not so much what the novel reveals in the creation of such doubles as what it conceals.

Moreover, this essay links the question of what the narrative conceals by providing doubles for itself to the issue of the connection between the novel and the social phenomena it purports to represent. Like all historical novels, *A Tale of Two Cities* advertises itself as a record of events that had their own separate existence outside of the novel. And like realist novels in general, it can accommodate a great deal of self-referentiality without relinquishing its claim to represent an independent reality. Indeed, *A Tale of Two Cities,* like many nineteenth-century novels, often achieves its self-reflectiveness just by calling

From *Dickens Studies Annual* 12 (1983). © 1983 by AMS Press, Inc.

attention to itself as mere representation. By presenting itself as simple representation, a thing whose very thingness is secondary or epiphenomenal, the novel conceals an aspect of itself; it conceals the fact that it is itself a kind of social practice. By drawing its content from social phenomena that are at once independent realities and analogues for novelistic narration, the novel gets us to focus alternately on what it is *about* and on how it accomplishes its representational effects. In the very act of giving us these alternative perspectives, the novel obscures its deeply social roots and functions. But the critic can uncover what the novel seeks to bury if she refuses to limit herself to the perspectives of the text itself, if she is willing to regard the novel as one among a number of historical phenomena, to investigate the separate but competing social functions of the novel and the phenomena it takes as its dark doubles.

The issue of analogues, metaphors, or doubles for narration and the issue of the social functions of fiction, then, are dealt with here as a single issue, an issue inseparable from larger topics in nineteenth-century social history. To demonstrate this unity, I will discuss three social phenomena that the narrative takes as analogues for itself precisely because they are in competition with the novel. The English public execution, the French Revolution, and the crime of resurrection, or grave robbing, are all internal analogues for the novel, but they are more than that; they are additionally alternatives to it, for they accomplish many of the novel's functions. By using them as internal, contrasting doubles for itself, by attempting to incorporate them, the novel tries to clear a space for itself, differentiate itself from the social and supersede it.

All of these phenomena—English public executions, the French Revolution, and the crime of resurrectionism—are presented in *A Tale of Two Cities* as monstrous violators of the realm of the private. As such, all might seem to threaten the very foundations of the nineteenth-century novel, a genre that grows out of and depends on a high valuation of the private and domestic realms. However, as violators of the private, these phenomena might also be said to *resemble* the novel, whose most basic task, as Dickens formulated it in the following well-known passage from *Dombey and Son,* was the exposure of the private. Here is the narrator of *Dombey and Son* invoking himself: "Oh for a good spirit who would take the house tops off, with a more potent and benignant hand than the lame demon in the tale, and show a Christian people what dark shapes issue from amidst their homes."

This longing for exposure and revelation, for the transgression of the very public/private boundary created and valued by the novel, can be detected everywhere in Dickens's novels. The wish to take the house-tops off, to render the private observable, is the wish informing the very existence of the omniscient narrator.

But the quotation from *Dombey and Son* presents this activity of the exposure of the private in two lights, one flattering and one very unflattering. Even as the narrator suggests that exposure can be the work of a good spirit, expelling hidden evils and creating light and order, he reminds us that it is nevertheless a transgression, and, conse-quently, within the novel's structure of values, akin to the work of a demon. How can the novel conceal this side of its own need to reveal and expose; how can the novelist reassure himself and his readers that he is in league with the good spirit, that his operations are benign? One way to suppress the fear that novelistic omniscience verges on the demonic is to provide, within the novel, an alternative version of the will to omniscience, one that is clearly destructive, preferably murder-ous or ghoulish, so that by contrast, the narrator's activities will seem restrained and salutary. Execution, the Revolution, and resurrectionism perform precisely this function in *A Tale of Two Cities*.

Consider, for example, the public execution, and consider it, for a moment, independently of the novel to get a sense of why Dickens was attracted to it. No event was better suited to render the private public, to expose the intimate in the interests of public order. In its most obvious sense, this would be true of all public executions, for by definition they expose to full public view a moment that was becom-ing more and more intensely private as the nineteenth-century wore on, the moment of fatal suffering and death. That exposure should remind us of the historical links between public executions and those other ritual inversions of public and private: human sacrifice and carni-val. Furthermore, when we consider the physical details of hanging, the type of execution used in England seems calculated to maximize the exposure of the dying victim. The erection of the penis and the evacuation of the bowels are among such details, and hanging, up until quite late in the Victorian period was a slow-working method; the drop was short, and the body was left, fully visible, to writhe and strangle for many minutes.

Moreover, as Dickens reminds us in *A Tale of Two Cities,* some crimes were punishable by even more intrusive forms of exposure. One of our earliest views of Charles Darnay renders him, through the ogreish anticipation of the crowd at his trial, a man literally turned inside out:

> The sort of interest with which this man was stared and breathed at, was not a sort that elevated humanity. Had he stood in peril of a less horrible sentence—had there been a chance of any one of its savage details being spared—by just so much would he have lost in his fascination. The form that was to be doomed to be so shamefully mangled, was the sight; the immortal creature that was to be so butchered and torn asunder, yielded the sensation.

Treason, you will recall, is the charge, and the penalty is an almost unimaginable mixing up of specular awareness and intense interiority, as the live sufferer is forced to watch the breaking open, pulling out and destruction of his own insides. To emphasize the extent of its violation, Dickens includes the full sentence:

> "Ah!" returned the man, with a relish; "he'll be drawn on a hurdle to be half hanged, and then he'll be cut down and sliced before his own face, and then his inside will be taken out and burnt while he looks on, and then his head will be chopped off, and he'll be cut into quarters. That's the sentence."

In these fairly obvious ways, then, the public execution, especially when accompanied by torture, can be seen as a nightmare of transparency, of publicly displaying what is hidden, intimate, secret, in the interests of creating social order and cohesion. Here is a collective longing for omniscience and power taking the most savage form imaginable. Here it is not just the walls or rooftops of the house that are ripped away, but the walls of the body itself. And thus Dickens's appalled references to several brutal executions at the outset of the novel establish the crucial differences between such practices and the novel's own will to transparency. Compared to the awful executions mentioned in chapter one and to Damiens's execution recounted later in detail, the novelist's methods of exposing the intimate are safe, sane, sanitary, and benevolent. They are safe because they do not entail that reversibility of violence dramatized in *A Tale of Two Cities*. As Michel Foucault has argued, penal reformers of the eighteenth and nineteenth centuries (and Dickens was such a reformer) feared that a population exposed to such a violent theater of punishment would become a

violent population. This note is sounded early in *A Tale of Two Cities,*
where we learn in the first chapter that the hangman's seemingly
arbitrary activities only contribute further to the disorder and violence
that can easily turn against the State, and keep turning and turning as
they do in Dickens's portrayal of the French Revolution.

In contrast, the novelist may pry, spy, and expose the secret, the
personal, but he manages to do these things while maintaining both
propriety and privacy. Indeed, the very production and consumption
of novels, as well as their contents, perpetuate the idea that the private
can be made public, brought to light, and yet still be kept private. In
this sense, Dickens's work as a novelist is of a piece with his work in
reforming the law. The public execution, he argues, should give way
to a procedure relying on a few witnesses and a lot of paperwork. As
Dickens describes the procedure in a letter to the *Times* in 1849, the
multitude of the crowd would be replaced by a multitude of pieces of
writing:

> To attend the execution I would summon a jury of 24, to be
> called the Witness Jury, eight to be summoned on a low
> qualification, eight on a higher; eight on a higher still; so
> that it might fairly represent all classes of society. There
> should be present likewise, the governor of the gaol, the
> chaplain, the surgeon and other officers. All these should
> sign a grave and solemn form of certificate (the same in
> every case) on such a day on such an hour, in such a gaol,
> for such a crime, such a murderer was hanged in their sight.
> There should be another certificate from the officers of the
> prison that the person hanged was that person and no other;
> a third that the person was buried.

As in the novel itself, in the private execution, as Dickens called his
imagined punishment, that which is private is given over to the power
of the public, but the public executes its power privately.

Thus, the very form of the novel defines itself against the public
execution, not only in spite of, but also because of their resemblances.
This is especially true in *A Tale of Two Cities,* which establishes the
public execution as one of its founding abominations. To take the
public execution merely as a point of departure, however, is to ignore
some of the more subtle ways in which the novel incorporates and
depends on the institution of the public execution. To explore these
further connections, I will need to discuss not the general institution of

public executions, but certain peculiarities of English public executions. Thus far I have been talking as if the execution, both inside and outside the novel, consisted merely in the forcible exposure of the intimate sensations of the condemned person's body, but the English execution did two other things particularly well that the novel was supposed to do: it retrospectively narrated an individual life while it simultaneously created a sense of social cohesion and totality.

English executions differed from those of other nations in the degree of activity allowed the victim and his opportunities for autobiographical representation. The victim's first such opportunity was his trial, but many opportunities succeeded condemnation. There was, for example, the theatrical opportunity provided by the prison chapel service that took place on the Sunday before the execution. Here the Ordinary of Newgate, the prison chaplain, would deliver a sermon, not only to the condemned, but also to the crowds of people who would bribe their way in to see the condemned. Because they had an audience, the prisoners were very often rowdy during this service, intent on expressing themselves, and the Ordinary's record is crowded with complaints: Christopher Freeman, we learn, "behaved very undecently, laughed and seemed to make a mock of everything that was serious and regular." And Ann Mudd, the account tells, "used to sing obscene songs, and talked very indecently," while Christopher Rawlings in the days before he was hanged busied himself in chapel by cutting off the tassels of the pulpit cushion. In addition to these small examples of self-dramatization, each condemned prisoner in Newgate was required to go through an autobiographical exercise. He was required to assist the Ordinary in making an *account* of his life. And there were frequently extraordinary struggles over these accounts. In the first place, the Ordinary as narrator often had difficulty subduing his rebellious characters. They would not always go along with his version of the plot. A historian of Newgate tells us,

> The Ordinary not only liked to have positive statements of guilt to the particular crime, but assent to a general range of immoral conduct. A story was told about Lorraine [an eighteenth-century Ordinary] and a young pickpocket about to be hanged. The Ordinary, expecting to hear the lad explain his sinful life in terms of Sabbath-breaking, lewd women or drink, was surprised when the boy insisted that

he was innocent of them all, particularly the first since as a pickpocket he could never afford to miss a Sunday.

In the second place, prisoners often wanted to sell their stories to higher bidders outside the prison walls. They wrote their own manuscripts in secret and smuggled them out to high-paying publishers. Other prisoners simply tried to keep their secret until they were on the scaffold, where their last speech would reveal all. But even before they got to the scaffold, in the days when hanging took place at Tyburn, there were ample opportunities for making speeches about one's life. The procession sometimes made several pub stops and stops to visit friends; the condemned would get down and drink and talk over old times. Both during these stops and during other parts of the journey, the condemned gave blessings, kissed their children goodbye, cursed people, etc. Executions, in short, could turn into enacted autobiographies, which were supplemented by the many accounts of the life and crimes of the condemned that were being sold all along the route and at the place of execution. Such life histories of criminals were, of course, the immediate ancestors of the novel.

English executions were also unique in the extent to which they obscured the power of the State. They seem staged to create the illusion that a total society, not a single class of government, was executing a felon. What is more, in the eighteenth and nineteenth centuries, the people were not content to be represented symbolically through the crown at these events, but turned out themselves in huge and generally disorderly crowds that were nevertheless socially differentiated. Indeed, we might argue that, in a time when a sense of social totality was becoming increasingly difficult to achieve, the public execution was a reassuring representation of wholeness. Nowhere else would all strata of society display themselves in such numbers. Tickets were sold, and the wealthy would pay high prices for gallery seats. At public executions one could see the differentiated but nevertheless cohesive whole of eighteenth- and nineteenth-century England.

The public execution, then, in addition to enacting a personal narrative also provided a synoptic view of society; the very two things the novel prided itself on doing. Indeed, the connection between the novelistic synoptic vision and the public hanging is explicit in a few of Dickens's novels. A famous early example of this connection is the death of Bill Sikes in *Oliver Twist*. Sikes's death admittedly is not technically an execution, but that makes it all the more revealing for my purposes, for it perfectly reproduces the submergence of the state in the English execution. It is the whole population of London, and not just the police, that brings Sikes to bay and causes him to hang himself—Sikes is on a rooftop attempting to let himself down, with a rope, into a ditch:

> The crowd had been hushed during these few moments, watching his motions and doubtful of his purpose, but the instant they perceived it and knew it was defeated, they raised a cry of triumphant execration to which all their previous shouting had been whispers. Again and again it rose. Those who were at too great a distance to know its meaning, took up the sound; it echoed and re-echoed; it seemed as though the whole city had poured its population out to curse him.
>
> On pressed the people from the front—on, on, on, in a strong struggling current of angry faces, with here and there a gathering torch to light them up, and show them out in all their wrath and passion. The houses on the opposite side of the ditch had been entered by the mob; sashes were thrown up, or torn bodily out; there were tiers and tiers of faces in every window; cluster upon cluster of people clinging to every house-top. Each little bridge (and there were three in sight) bent beneath the weight of the crowd upon it. Still the current poured on to find some nook or hole from which to vent their shouts, and only for an instant see the wretch.

This is the only time in the novel that the divided world of the metropolis achieves wholeness, for Harry Maylie and Mr. Brownlow are parts of the mob, which also includes the poor and the criminal. As in *Dombey and Son,* the rooftop here is the perch of omniscience, but the synoptic moment is created and perceived only in the seconds before hanging.

Dickens also uses the moment of execution as the synoptic moment in *A Tale of Two Cities.* Here again the omniscience gained in the moment of Sydney Carton's execution, a prophetic vision giving us a chronological panorama extending several generations into the future, is synonymous with the narrator's omniscience.

In sum, Dickens uses the public execution as a method of defining, by contrast, the innocence of his own longing for transparency and omniscience. However, he then incorporates the conventions of representation of the English execution into his narrative to achieve some of his most typically novelistic effects: the retrospective of Sydney Carton's life, for example, and the prophetic synopsis of its close. This incorporation, indeed, is an effort to absorb the functions of the public execution and circumscribe them within the novel. In the same letter to the *Times* in which Dickens requested that the crowd be replaced by its representatives (eight men from each social class) at executions, he expressed his hostility toward the theatrically autobiographical character of public executions. He recommends that all elements of public entertainment be suppressed:

> [The] execution within the walls of the prison should be conducted with every terrible solemnity that careful consideration could devise. Mr. Calcraft the hangman . . . should be restrained in his unseemly briskness, in his jokes, his oaths, and his brandy.

Moreover, even journalistic accounts publicizing the condemned are to be disallowed:

> From the moment of a murderer being sentenced to death, I would dismiss him to dread obscurity. . . . I would allow no curious visitors to hold any communication with him; I would place every obstacle in the way of his sayings and doings being served up in print on Sunday for the perusal of families.

The novelist, alone, it seems, should be able to appropriate, through representation, the functions of the execution.

In the paradoxical nature of its relationship to public executions— the way it at once uses them as a point of departure and contrast to itself and also incorporates them to achieve its own internal purposes—*A Tale of Two Cities* resembles a second historical phenomenon that is analogous to novelistic narration: the French Revolution. Like the narrator, the revolutionaries take the outrages of public execution as founding events, events that are to justify them and differentiate them from the Old Regime. The execution of Damiens and that of the Marquis's assassin are particularly important in this regard. Finally, however, the Revolution becomes even more dependent on the public execution than the Old Regime had been. If the public execution is a nightmare of omniscience, of the exposure of the private to public scrutiny, then the Revolution is that nightmare amplified a thousand times. And this amplification can be seen and felt not only in the multiplication of executions but also in the numerous invasions and expositions of the private that characterize the Revolution from the outset and link it closely to the method of narrative omniscience.

The secret brotherhood of the Jacquerie resists the intrusion of royalist spies, but it also creates itself through spying, through the surveillance and exposure of dark things and private things. "Do you make a show of Monsieur Manette?" asked Mr. Lorry of Defarge when they discover the three Jacques "looking into the room" of the distraught doctor "through some chinks or holes in the wall." "I show him, in the way you have seen, to a chosen few," replies Defarge. Indeed, the intrusive stare characterizes most personifications of the incipient Revolution. One such personification is Madame Defarge, who always "looks steadily" at the people she enters in her knitted record. It is the stare that differentiates her from other denizens of St. Antoine:

> So cowed was their condition, and so long and hard their experience of what such a man [as the Marquis] could do to them, within the law and beyond it, that not a voice, or a hand, or even an eye was raised. Among the men, not one. But the women who stood knitting looked up steadily, and looked the Marquis in the face.

A second personification of the embryonic revolution is the Gorgon, who, we are told, "surveys" the country house of the Evrémondes, turning the Marquis to stone. Whereas the Gorgon of mythology is a creature who kills by being looked at, the Gorgon-Jacquerie kills its victims by looking at them. By inverting the myth here, Dickens merely emphasizes the significance of the stare.

Once the Revolution establishes itself, the stare becomes a national characteristic. A whole population practices surveillance on itself, a surveillance that ultimately destroys. When Darnay returns to France, he encounters, we are told several times, a "universal watchfulness" that the narrator finds particularly abhorrent, just as he deplores the exposure of the domestic encoded in the law demanding that all the names of the inhabitants of a residence be listed outside on the front of the house. Indeed, these demands for transparency, for the exhibition of the private, are excessive. It is as if the Revolution had inspired every citizen with a need to rip away the house-tops, to expose the interior, in short, to commit the transgressions of the omniscient narrator.

Both the Revolution and the Dickens narrator need to transgress against the private, and, to justify their transgression, they must create a belief that dark things (plots, conspiracies, vices) lurk everywhere, needing to be revealed. The belief in secrets creates the need to expose, but the need to expose is reciprocally dependent on the invention of secret plots. The French Revolution was uncannily like a Dickens novel in this regard: the invented hidden plot justifies the will to omniscience.

Dickens, of course, did not invent this characterization of the French Revolution, which had already been represented, by anti-revolutionaries and revolutionaries alike, as a practice of excessive exposure. In his *Reflections on the Revolution in France,* for example, Edmund Burke characterizes revolutionary thought as a process of unmasking, unclothing, stripping away symbolic drapery:

> All the decent Drapery of life is to be rudely torn off. All the superadded ideas, furnished from the wardrobe of a moral imagination, which the heart owns, and the understanding ratifies, as necessary to cover the defects of our shivering naked nature, and to raise it to dignity in our own estimation, are to be exploded as a ridiculous, absurd, and antiquated fashion.

And Carlyle, whose constant concern is with the making and unmaking of symbols also notes the rending and discarding of the old symbolic vestures in revolutionary activity. The revolutionary symbols that replace the symbols of the Old Regime, moreover, are often symbols representing the pulling away of symbols: the destruction of the Bastille, decapitated heads of aristocrats, the guillotine itself.

These representations of the Revolution as exposure, we must note, were also the self-representations of the Revolution, especially just before and during the time of the Terror. The Terror explicated the Revolution's insistence on transparency and its corollary invention of hidden plots. Revolutionaries had always expressed a great deal of anxiety about secrets, about privacy itself and about language in general, which they saw as a primary tool of deception. There were constant demands for the perfectly expressive and revealing word. And as Radicals gained more and more power, they predicated the very survival of the Revolution on, as a historian of the Revolution puts it,

> transparency between citizen and citizen, between the citizens and their government, between the individual and

general will. . . . This kind of transparency gave meaning to the civic oath and to the revolutionary festival, both of which depended on enthusiastic adherence, i.e., on the abolition of distance between citizen and citizen and between individual and community. Community, in essence, *was* this transparency between citizens.

> (Lynn A. Hunt, "The Rhetoric of Revolution in France,"
> *History Workshop Journal* 15 [1983])

This was the mentality that led, during the Terror, to the institutionalization of public vigilance, denunciation, and decapitation, the essence of the revolutionary experience as we see it depicted in *A Tale of Two Cities*. The idea that secret plots were lurking everywhere was, of course, necessary to justify this vigilance, and the more transparent the community became, the more nefarious must these plots be, for authorized enclaves of privacy had been wiped out. The fact that these plots were invisible, even given this new transparency, was proof of their pernicious purposes. Thus when Saint-Just denounces Danton, whose crime is the concealment of a network of plotters, he stresses the fact that guilt is proved by the burial of evidence: "You will recognize," he exclaims, "the sure signs of the party opposed to the Revolution, the party which always conceals itself." In other words, the fact that you cannot see it proves that it is there. How can it be a plot if it is not hidden?

The resemblances to Dickens's novels, with their insistence on omniscience and their concomitant need for someone always to be hiding something, are obvious. Moreover, these characteristics are not unique to Dickens; it is practically a *donnée* of nineteenth-century realist fiction that the real is beneath the surface, a hidden network of connection that must remain at least partially hidden if the novel is to continue. When full transparency is achieved, the novel ends. When we know all the connections between the Evrémondes, the Manettes and the Defarges, the novel no longer has a raison d'être. On his late-night ramble through Paris, just before he goes to La Force to change places with Darnay, Sydney Carton hears the final revelation, makes the final connection between Madame Defarge and the Evrémondes. At that moment there is nothing left to be learned; the novel, like Carton, has reached the threshold of full execution. It must end, for its continuation is as dependent on the discovery of plots as is that of the revolution itself.

It was just such an end to their own raison d'être that the Radicals feared, and thus they set themselves the task of the infinite invention and discovery of plots. Hence the Revolution reminds us of that reluctance to end that so often characterizes the Victorian novel. Revolution is opposed to resolution: it is a kind of fiction in which ultimate climax must be always deferred. Saint-Just comments on the infinitude of the structure he is creating: "One speaks of the highpoint of the revolution; who will fix it, this highpoint? It is moving."

But novels, of course, must bring themselves to an end; they must move more or less purposely, willfully toward resolution. *A Tale of Two Cities,* indeed, emphasizes this difference between itself and the revolution by merging its own execution, its own ending, with Carton's execution and thereby stressing the voluntariness of its close. And this impulse toward resolution is only one of the most obvious ways in which the novel distinguishes its own practices from those of the Revolution. The differences are, after all, the point of the comparison. The Revolution, like the public execution, is a double for the narration itself in all of the ways I have just detailed. But like the other doublings in this book, indeed like splitting and pairing in general, the doubling of the methods of novelistic narration with the methods of the Revolution is a protective device. Sydney Carton saves Charles Darnay by a set of resemblances and differences that allow the displacement of one by the other. Earlier, in the London trial episode, casting suspicion on Sydney Carton draws off suspicion from Charles Darnay. Similarly, the presence of the Revolution as a double of the novelistic narration exculpates the narration. By depicting this excessive, malignant, demonic version of the will to transparency, the Revolution, the novel discovers itself to be, in comparison, moderate, benign, even angelic.

Thus we are never confused about whether the novel is for or against the protection of the domestic enclave it exposes. The novelist makes his revelation of the private in the name of the private and for the sake of the private. The Revolution is a specific attack upon the private by means of exposure. In contradistinction, the novel seems to represent the repulsion of that attack. We do not readily suspect the narrator of exercising or desiring any excessive power over his universe or over us. The narrator sees and detects, not for his own profit (like the many spies in the book), but supposedly for the profit of the good people he spies on.

His detection resembles the businesslike spying of Jarvis Lorry. As Lorry interrogates Miss Pross about Doctor Manette's past, he reminds her that he and she are "both people of business." And at several other points during their interview, he recalls her to a sense of his serious but benign intentions. "I don't approach the topic with you out of curiosity, but out of zealous interest," he assures her; and he continues, "a doubt lurks in my mind, Miss Pross, whether it is good for Doctor Manette to have that suppression always shut up within him. Indeed, it is this doubt and the uneasiness it sometimes causes me that has led me to our present confidence." Both the revolutionaries and Jarvis Lorry are intent on discovering the secret of Doctor Manette's imprisonment, yet Jarvis Lorry's prying seems pure and benign to us. We have no trouble believing him when he tells us it is for Doctor Manette's good. Similarly, we are sure that what the narrative as a whole reveals, it reveals for the good of the exposed. We do not suspect the narrative, and we do not suspect it because its double, the Revolution, so theatrically exhibits all the suspicious behavior associated with compulsive prying.

The Revolution exhibits this behavior theatrically, and Jerry Cruncher, the resurrection man, exhibits it surreptitiously, drawing off and disposing of any residual uneasiness we might feel about the narrator's discreet and businesslike procedures. The crime of resurrectionism, as A. D. Hutter has shown . . . , is the clearest and the most elaborate of the narrative's dark doubles for itself. Hutter has pointed out that Jerry's job is like the narrator's in that both dig up the past and uncover buried mysteries. Jerry's work is also like the narrator's, however, in that both expose the private place. Robbing a grave is, after all, yet another version of pulling off a rooftop. And, indeed, the crime of resurrectionism was often represented as the ultimate violation of privacy, the privacy of both the dead and the family. It was a crime against family sentiment, the very foundation of the domestic. This is particularly clear when the robbing of a woman's grave is reported. The following account of the activities of Edinburgh medical students illustrates the depth of popular feeling on this subject:

> Rosyth was the scene of another tragic story in which Edinburgh students were concerned. They had learned of the death of a beautiful young bride in her first childbirth. Insensible to all considerations save the gratification of their passion for dissection, they had made it a matter of competition who should obtain possession of the body of the village belle. The party that reached the spot first set to work with

all speed and soon had the body unearthed and stripped preparatory to placing it in the sack for removal. They had paused for a moment to admire the perfect proportions and fair skin of the female form divine that lay before them when the sound of a dog howling in distress fell on their ears. Presently the light of a lantern warned them that some-one was approaching, and without waiting to put the body in the sack and shoulder the burden, they seized it by the heels and fled, dragging it along the ground behind them. When they reached the sea wall beyond which their boat lay in readiness at the edge of the tide, the woman's long, golden hair, which in life had reached below her knees when uncoiled, and loosened in the exhumation had trailed out as the body was drawn along, became entangled among the rough, projecting stones, and stayed their progress. Tug-ging violently, they overcame the obstruction and reached the boat with their freight, but in their tugging some of the golden tresses and part of the scalp had been torn away, and were left entangled in the sea wall. The husband, who had been alarmed by the uneasy howling of his dead wife's pet, and had set out to assure himself that her grave had not been disturbed, was diverted from his first intention by the sound of the students' hurried flight and turned in pursuit. When he came to the sea wall the faithful animal, which had followed him, scented these remains and stood barking ex-citedly over them. By the light of his lantern he recognized the fair hair that but a year before had been garlanded with orange blossoms and now brought him confirmation of his worst fears. As the students drew away from the shore, congratulating themselves on having beaten their competi-tors, he stood upon the wall holding to his quivering lips all that was left to him of his bride, so beautiful even in death, and calling down the vengeance of Heaven on the violators of her last sanctuary.

What strikes one immediately about this powerful little narrative is the ingenuousness of the writer's claim that the medical students are "insensible to all considerations save the gratification of their passion for dissection" even as the very next clause in the sentence stresses the overtly sexual dimension of this passion. The passion for dissection, which leads to resurrectionism, is so closely associated with sexual violation in the narrator's mind that he assumes the former entails the latter. Nor does the narrator seem aware that there is any tension between his conventional, romantic language and the fact that the abducted woman is a corpse. We are, for example, left with the standard sentimental image of the young husband pressing his stolen bride's "golden tresses" to his lips, and are expected not to flinch at the bizarre detail that bits of scalp are dangling from those tresses. Such discordant elements are only conceivable within an ideology that already, in some sense, conceives of the domestic woman as so immobile, passive, and sequestered that she is already dead and buried. In violating her grave, the resurrectionists transgress against the culmination of her privacy, the perfection of her feminine being; they are "the violators of her *last* sanctuary."

Much less violent, of course, is the sort of violation practiced by the novel, but we should remember Miss Pross's complaint that ever since the Resurrection of the Doctor, that is, since the opening of the novel, "hundreds of people who are not at all worthy of Ladybird [have] come here looking after her." We are, of course, supposed to see Miss Pross's complaint as absurd and fantastic; Lucie's sanctuary has been invaded, not by hundreds of people, but by half a dozen; she has only three men desiring her body, not throngs. Nevertheless, our first tour of the Manettes' home is conducted in a strangely guilt-ridden fashion. Mr. Lorry, who had previously "resurrected" the doctor, arrives at their "secluded" retreat when no one is home, and, with a strong consciousness of his own (licensed) invasiveness, wanders from room to room, allowing the narrator to comment on what each room reveals of the inhabitants, especially of Lucie. Later we see this tour as part of Lorry's attempt to retrieve the doctor's past, an attempt at yet another benign resurrection. Nevertheless, the slight taint of prying remains attached to our introduction into Lucie's house, giving a certain limited credence to Miss Pross's alarm: we are the "hundreds of people."

Jerry Cruncher's domestic establishment provides a comic inversion of this suppressed connection between the crime of resurrectionism and the exposure of the domestic. Jerry, whose acts of exposure are themselves clandestine, can tolerate no revelations within his own household. He continually abuses his wife for praying, for communicating with a potentially interfering Being. He tries to beat his wife into protecting his privacy, into concealing it from an omniscient gaze.

The outlandishness of Jerry's claim to speak in the name of privacy and the inviolability of the family circle overshadows the illegitimacy of the narrator's similar claim.

Of all the doubles for novelistic narration in *A Tale of Two Cities,* then, the crime of resurrectionism is in many ways the most comprehensive. And, of course, it is also a close relative to the two other doubles I have discussed here, providing historical as well as metaphorical links between them. Hutter mentioned its connections to the French Revolution's secularism and anti-historical impulses as well as its parodic relationship to the theme of *liberté.* Another of its connections to the Revolution is simply the historical fact that that event brought in the method of teaching anatomy that first created the lucrative market in bodies in England and Scotland.

But there is yet another link between the Revolution and the crime of resurrection established through their common association with execution. Like the Revolution, resurrection destroys the distinction between the innocent and the guilty. It demands the exposure alike of those who deserve it and those who do not. Prior to the English Anatomy Act of 1832, the only bodies legally available for dissection were those of executed criminals. To be dissected was to be treated like a criminal; indeed, it was to be treated like the worst kind of criminal. Even hardened convicts on their way to the gallows begged not to be sent to the Surgeons. One Vincent Davis, for example, who was hanged at Tyburn in 1725 for killing his wife, exclaimed on arrest, "I have killed the best wife in the world, and I am certain of being hanged, but for God's sake, don't let me be anatomised!" Dissection was a fate then reserved only for the most despised or unfortunate of the condemned. But the resurrection men broke through this reservation. Treating the bodies of the most innocent like those of murderers, they provided a postmortem Reign of Terror.

Resurrection, then, as a double for omniscient narration, is both historically and metaphorically linked to those other narrative analogues, revolution and execution. Indeed, by its wealth of associations it seems to absorb the others. But at the same time, resurrection is in competition with both execution and revolution. An executed body, after all, did not need to be resurrected; it was free to the surgeons for public dissection. And, of course, the punishment for drawing and quartering, as Jerry interestedly points out, "spiles" the body. Spoils it, that is, for dissection by dissecting it alive. Jerry greatly resents this destruction of prospective "scientific goods." But he resents even more the surplus of bodies created by the Terror. When he renounces the trade of resurrectionism, he explains to Jarvis Lorry, "A man don't see all this here goin' on dreadful round him, in the way of Subjects without heads, dear me, plentiful enough fur to bring the price down to porterage and hardly that, without havin' his serious thoughts of things." Behind Jerry's conversion from grave robber to grave digger is the understanding that revolutionary society would ruin his trade. A society not based on family sentiment, the respect for privacy, and the sanctity of the domestic would flood the market with bodies, and the "honest tradesman" would be out of business. Resurrectionism, like the novel, needs the respect for privacy it violates; it relies on having things buried.

Resurrection, then, gives us an analogue for narration, but also a double for the antagonistic, competitive relationship between the novel and its analogues. Neither the novel nor the resurrectionist could survive in a society where exposure was cheap, plentiful, even, God forbid, free. How can the honest tradesman, the resurrectionist and the novelist, thrive in a society that turns itself inside out? Resurrection, then, is more than just *another* double for narration; it also doubles the novel's competitive relationship to the theatrical doubles (execution and Revolution) that we examined earlier.

The displacement of resurrection by execution is an inverted version of the displacement of execution and Revolution by the novel. And inversion, of course, is the point. One of the neatest tricks of *A Tale of Two Cities* is its creation of the illusion that a theatrical society is displacing the honest tradesman; whereas, of course, the opposite was the case: the honest tradesman, the novelist, privately selling his discreetly packaged revelations of the private, was displacing the theatrical society. And he could only do so by advertising the inviolability of the private. Thus, the narrator's only first-person statement can be read, not as a poignant lament about the ultimate inaccessibility of one's intimates, but as a reassurance that the private will always be there and yet will always be just beyond our full comprehension:

> A wonderful fact to reflect upon, that every human creature
> is constituted to be that profound secret and mystery to
> every other. A solemn consideration, when I enter a great
> city by night, that every one of those darkly clustered houses
> encloses its own secret; that every room in every one of
> them encloses its own secret; that every beating heart in the

hundreds of thousands of breasts there, is in some of its imaginings, a secret to the heart nearest it! Something of the awfulness, even of Death itself, is referable to this. . . . My friend is dead, my neighbor is dead, my love, the darling of my soul, is dead; it is the inexorable consolation and perpetuation of the secret that was always in that individuality, and which I shall carry in mine to my life's end. In any of the burial-places of this city through which I pass, is there a sleeper more inscrutable than its busy inhabitants are, in their innermost personality, to me, or than I am to them?

The quotation, which connects the narrator and the resurrection man by equating the domestic with the grave, posits a perpetual scarcity of intimate knowledge, and thereby raises the value of the revelation of the private, insuring a continued demand for the honest tradesman's goods.

As a double for both novelistic narration and the antagonistic relationship between novelistic narration and its doubles, resurrection is very revealing. Indeed, for the purposes of this essay, it is almost too revealing; this essay began with the premise that doubling is primarily a method for protecting and concealing, and yet here resurrection seems to be revealing the fact that the novel is actually in competition with the social practices it represents.

This revelation, however, is anything but automatic; it can be reached only by stripping away, with the aid of other historical materials, layers of concealment. The most proximate layer is the inversion just referred to: the inversion by which the private tradesman gets replaced by the theatrical society instead of, as in the case of the novelist, replacing that society. But even this inversion is screened from view by yet another act of doubling in which the theme of resurrection itself becomes an explicit double for doubling. That is, we do not see that resurrection is an ironic double for the competition between the novel and other social practices because the narrator introduces it as already doubled: it is the explicit ironic inversion of transcendent Resurrection with a capital "R" in the stories of Manette, Darnay and Carton. Resurrection comes into the novel, as it were, pre-paired with the very operation the novel advertises as its explicit analogue: benign Resurrection, which saves Doctor Manette, Charles Darnay, and Sydney Carton, which recalls to life, recollects the past, redeems the present and the future.

This explicit doubling of resurrection does two things. First it creates an illusion of candid self-referentiality: a book so explicit about its structure must have nothing to hide. What, after all, could be more honest than calling attention to one's own duplicity? Second, by explicitly pairing resurrectionism with the benign, angelic side of the will to omniscience, the narration controls and limits the similarities we will see between resurrection and the novel. Specifically, it suppresses the insight we have gained only by going outside the novel: the insight that the novelist and the resurrection man are both, out of self-interest, antagonistic to the theatrical society.

A Tale of Two Cities, then, not only gives us doubles of narration to draw suspicion away from itself, but it also gives us a double of doubling so that, if we restricted ourselves to the text, we could not possibly be suspicious of that method. Consequently, in *A Tale of Two Cities* we have a clear illustration of how omniscient, novelistic narration came to replace certain social practices of an earlier, more theatrical society by temporarily assuming some essential functions of those practices and then making itself an explicit contrast to them. Of all nineteenth-century novelists, Dickens may have been the most aware of the close bond between his own works and the more public and theatrical practices they were replacing. That may, in fact, be why we find in his work the cleverest mechanisms of concealment. The mechanisms need to be clever, for the thing being concealed is, in some ways, very obvious. The novel does not just record a social transition; it enacts one.

That transition was perhaps most powerfully enacted, paradoxically, on the Victorian stage itself, where Dickens, in the last years of his life, added a new item to his repertoire of public readings. He began doing the murder of Nancy and death of Bill Sikes from *Oliver Twist,* and he reported that the performances bore a strong resemblance to public executions: "There was a fixed expression of horror of me, all over the theatre, which could not have been surpassed if I had been going to be hanged. . . . It is quite a new sensation to be executed with that unanimity." How can this final institutional exchange be explained? Was Dickens giving back to the public, theatrical realm much of what he had appropriated from it? Were these readings public confessions, disclosures of the novelist's guilty connection to the phenomena he was displacing, as well as acts of reparation?

In answer to the first question, it must be pointed out that Dickens is here entering the realm of the theatrical, but only, after all, to modify it in the direction of the novelistic. His readings in general made a peculiarly non-theatrical use of the theater: with most of the stage darkened and draped, the solitary reader stood at the velvet-covered lectern reading the already familiar stories. No characters appeared, no scenes became visible; all was represented in words, realized only privately through the imaginative effort of each of the thousands of hearers. No theater could have been less like that normally experienced by Victorian theatergoers, who, amid noisy and unruly crowds, generally witnessed almost wordless productions of spectacular materiality, such as the real horses and chariots raced on conveyor belts in Victorian productions of *Ben Hur*. Given the nature of Victorian theater, when Dickens takes the stage to read his novels, we might say that he is blotting out the theatrical, making the stage a huge blankness to accommodate the resonating words of the novel. Far from being a capitulation to theatrical modes of representation, then, Dickens's readings can be seen as further acts of appropriation and displacement.

From this understanding of the readings in general, we may be able to derive the meaning of the violent *Oliver Twist* performances, which Dickens thought bore such a long likeness to public executions. As in all of Dickens's readings, the performance called attention to its novelistic representational mode; there was no stage illusion. The simulated self-execution of Sikes took place only in the private space of the hearers' minds, while the shared experiences were of Dickens's voice and the spectacle of his self-presentation as narrator. The revelation here is of the novelist, not of the executed. In his performance, Dickens does not directly pretend to be Bill Sikes; he does not even take the risk of identification taken by a normal actor. Instead, Dickens plays the novelist, exposes himself as novelist. It is the anonymous revealer who is here revealed. Consequently, in these performances, the novelist proves that he is willing to expose himself, and his exposures of others are thus justified. He is no furtive resurrection man, but a self-presenting representer.

Like Sydney Carton and Christ himself, the good Resurrection Men, Dickens experiences the execration of the crowd only as the self-conscious representer of another, but in Dickens's case the knowledge of the merely representational nature of the performance is, apparently, shared by performer and audience. However, underneath his self-conscious and candid representing that constantly calls attention to its mediations, a real self-execution was secretly taking place.

For Dickens had been told by his doctor and many of his friends that he was bringing his illness to a fatal crisis by performing the violent readings from *Oliver Twist*. And yet he willfully continued the performances even though he seems to have believed they would kill him. Concealing this self-executing Dickens is his criminal double, the self-executing Sikes. Far from being a public execution, these readings, which are the representation of a public execution, are also its inversion, the final triumph of the novelistic. No one's death is exposed here. Someone is dying, but only secretly, while the crowd's attention is focused on the duplicitous representation of the death of the double.

Indeed, Dickens uses the same methods of revelation and concealment when, in the guise of longing for the cessation of these performances, he longs for his own death and the final blankness of the theater. In a sentence that necessarily conjures the ghost of Sydney Carton, he writes of his last readings, " 'Like lights in a theater, they are being snuffed out fast,' as Carlyle says of the guillotined in his Revolution. I suppose I shall be glad when they are all snuffed out."

Charles Darnay
and Revolutionary Identity

Edwin M. Eigner

Since this essay is in some senses a continuation of a piece I published in *Dickens Studies Annual* 11 ("The Absent Clown in *Great Expectations*"), and since that piece contains the framework within which the following argument must be understood, I shall begin, as the RSC does at the beginning of each act of *Nicholas Nickleby,* with a brief recapitulation. The controlling idea in the first paper, as in this one, is that from as early as his own version of *Nicholas Nickleby* in 1838, Dickens structured each of his novels on a form of popular entertainment called the Christmas or Easter Pantomime.

Dickens's Pantomime is not to be confused either with the sort of thing Marcel Marceau does or with the cheap entertainments called pantomimes or pantos which are staged these days in England every Christmas season, although both are descendants. The Regency and Early Victorian Pantomime which influenced Dickens was a highly stylized affair, always in two parts. In the first and relatively realistic scene, a pair of young lovers would have their romantic plans frustrated by three characters: the girl's avaricious or weak father, a wicked or foppish lover whom the father favors, and a blundering comic servant. When the wicked lover seems about to triumph, a benevolent spirit out of Mother Goose or the Arabian Nights or some other fantasy appears and changes each of the characters into one of the figures from the English development of the *commedia dell'arte* Harlequinade. The girl becomes Columbine, the boy she loves becomes Harlequin, the father is changed to Pantaloon, the wicked lover is

From *Dickens Studies Annual* 12 (1983). © 1983 by AMS Press, Inc.

transformed to a figure called Dandy Lover, and the servant becomes Clown, who is the ancestor of Charles Chaplin and the circus and rodeo clowns of today. These transformations give the young lovers another chance, with the odds in their favor this time, for Harlequin is nimbler than his enemies and he is aided by a magic bat or slap-stick. He is also the beneficiary of the actions of Clown, who either intentionally or inadvertently betrays his masters, Pantaloon and Dandy Lover, and saves the young people. This is done at his own expense, not only because he receives blows from his master but, frequently, because he is himself in love with Columbine.

My argument is that most Dickens heroines find themselves surrounded by four would-be lovers, who correspond to the four male figures in the Harlequinade. She always has a father or a father figure who gets her into trouble, sometimes by selfishly exploiting her, as in *Nicholas Nickleby,* but more often unintentionally, as with Dr. Manette in *A Tale of Two Cities,* or at least without any consciously wicked intention. I make this last qualification because there is frequently the suggestion, as with Manette again, that the father's feeling for his daughter is not purely parental and that he views her favored lover, Charles Darnay in this novel, with more than a touch of sexual jealousy. Consciously, Manette means nothing but good for Charles, and he is sincerely active in his attempts to free him, but the efforts fail, after all, and it is, of course, Manette's testimony, written in the Bastille, which condemns Charles.

The heroine has also a wicked lover, whose principal crime is usually an aspiration to rise in the social world by unfair or crass means until he achieves the bliss of winning her. Lawyer Stryver of *A Tale of Two Cities* is a weak embodiment of this figure from the Dickens Pantomime. A more recognizable wicked lover is Carker the Manager of *Dombey and Son* or Uriah Heep of *David Copperfield,* of whom George Orwell writes:

> Considering how Heep's general lowness—his servile manners, dropped aitches and so forth—has been rubbed in throughout the book, there is not much doubt about the nature of Dickens's feelings. Heep, of course, is playing a villainous part, but even villains have sexual lives; it is the thought of the "pure" Agnes in bed with a man who drops his aitches that really revolts Dickens.

Stryver is like these wicked lovers because he perceives the heroine as the reward, not as the means of his elevation—he is rather proud, in fact, of his decision to please himself and marry a poor girl. He is also like the others in that his shouldering self-assertiveness and vulgar determination to rise in life represent or reflect a chief evil which the novel exposes. From one point of view, at least, social mobility at any price is what the French Revolution is all about.

Stryver is typical of this figure once again in that he employs, in a virtual slave capacity, the most dissipated and improvident of all the characters of the novel, a personage whom no one regards seriously and from whom no one ever expects anything, but who, like the Clown in the Harlequinade, always performs the essential action which saves the heroine. It was this character, developed from Newman Noggs of *Nicholas Nickleby*, through Micawber of *David Copperfield,* and finding most serious expression in Sydney Carton of *A Tale of Two Cities,* which I concentrated on in my paper of last year, arguing that since he possessed the Saturnalian or sexual energy which belonged in the Pantomime Harlequinade to Clown rather than Harlequin, he was able to act where the romantic lover, from whom one would naturally expect action, was powerless. David Copperfield cannot save Agnes from Uriah Heep, but Micawber can. In *Great Expectations,* where for the first time Dickens did not provide an adequate clown figure, the heroine is not rescued and actually marries and is bedded by the wicked lover. And in *A Tale of Two Cities* it is the unregarded Sydney Carton who can act decisively in the crisis, while his much more successful and substantial rival, Charles Darnay, has been powerless, powerless not only to defend himself from the revengeful fury of the revolution, but also impotent to protect his family, to avoid being caught in the machinations of his wicked uncle, to benefit the starving peasants on his French estate, and, perhaps most significantly, to carry out the first charge of his life, laid upon him by his mother when he was a boy, to find and care for the sister of the raped girl, Madame Defarge, who has little trouble finding and taking care of him.

It is this figure, the romantic lover, on whom I wish to concentrate this time, for just as Sydney Carton was the least funny and the most significant of Dickens's Clowns, so Charles Darnay is the most heavy-footed and, certainly to this point of the author's career, the most problematic of his Harlequins.

Readers and critics, until recently, at any rate, have found Dickens's romantic heroes among the least interesting of his characters, and

Darnay is certainly no exception in this regard. He has differed from the other heroes who end up with the girls, however, in that, from the beginning, and in spite of the facts that his manners are impeccable and usually calculated not to give offense, he has inspired animosity both from those within the novel and those outside it. If we could forgive the Wicked Marquis de St. Evrémonde anything, perhaps it would be for what Albert Hutter, in a brilliant essay, calls, his "murderous impulses towards his brother's child," for Charles holds himself morally superior to his uncle and openly rejects everything the latter stands for. This is, I believe, the only time in the novel he takes such a tone. Nevertheless, it is understandable, I suppose, that Madame Defarge and the revolutionaries should see Charles, whether mistakenly or not, as their enemy, the symbol of their oppression. Even the Old Bailey crowd in England can perhaps be excused for their disappointment at not getting to see him half-hanged, then taken down and sliced before his own face, then have his insides burnt while he looks on, then have his head chopped off, and then have his body cut into quarters. Maybe there is not anything personal in this. One could not hope, moreover, that Charles would be especially popular with his English romantic rivals. It is to be expected, therefore, that Stryver should "believe there is contamination in such a scoundrel" and that Carton should simply "hate the fellow." Nor should we be surprised at the negative feelings of those millions of readers who have identified with Carton and felt his rejection by Lucie as if it were their own. Even Charles is quick to excuse his father-in-law for condemning him and his descendants "to the last of their race." It's what he's come to expect. Nevertheless, some of the dislike for Darnay goes beyond the explanations provided.

Less than a month after the last chapter of the novel was published, James Fitzjames Stephen wrote to express his contempt for this coward who "thought he had better live by his wits in London than have the responsibility of continuing a landowner in France," and Lawrence Frank, a recent interpreter, sees Charles as a self-deceiver, who "lives 'unknown in England,' where he is 'no Marquis': unknown to his tenants in France, unknown to his wife, unknown, finally, to himself." In the centennial year of Dickens's death, 1970, the French critic Sylvère Monod noted the "unusually unanimous critical feeling against" Darnay, citing the condemnations of John Gross, K. J. Fielding, and Edgar Johnson. He concludes the summary with his own conviction that while Dickens identified Darnay with himself, "lending him his own leaning towards 'The Loadstone Rock,' " he did not give Darnay "more than .01 percent" of his own vitality.

Jack Lindsay was, I believe, the first to note this identification of Dickens with Darnay when he pointed out that the latter "has the revealing initials Charles D." Charles's real name, Evrémonde, has also been seen as significant, but in an almost opposite way. Robert Alter believes it suggests the character is "a sort of Everyman," and Elliot Gilbert, in a paper delivered at the 1982 Santa Cruz Dickens Conference and printed in [Dickens Studies Annual], calls the name "a multi-lingual, two-cities pun on 'everyman' or 'all-the-world.' " At another paper delivered at the same conference, Garrett Stewart emphasized the sudden grammatical shift into the first-person plural in book 3, chapter 13. The reader, as Stewart suggested, is virtually "conscripted" to accompany the drugged Darnay as the coach takes him, Mr. Lorry, Dr. Manette, and the two Lucies away from the danger of Paris.

Perhaps these insights, beginning with Alter's, provide clues to Darnay's unpopularity. If Dickens wants to identify such a character with himself, that is one matter; but if he is going to try to force us to accept such an identification, that is something else again. But why should we object? Charles is good-looking, well-born, well-bred, well-educated, intelligent, fortunate in both life and love. If he does not have Charles Dickens's vitality, he at least has his industry, and if the aristocratic Fitzjames Stephen wants to call schoolteaching "living by one's wits," why should literary critics, who are most of them schoolteachers themselves, want to share the contempt?

I think an answer to this question and also to the question of why Charles is so disliked within the novel may lie in the way this hero regards himself. Darnay's self-contempt is not so Byronically obvious as Carton's, but I suspect it is deeper and more difficult to transcend, at least by his own efforts. Think, for instance, of the meek way he accepts Carton's insolence after the English trial and the modest way he presses his claim to Lucie when he asks her father not to oppose his courtship.

> I have felt [he says], and do feel even now, that to bring my love—even mine—between you [and Lucie], is to touch your history with something not quite so good as itself.

At the level of the book's religious allegory, he is, of course, Everyman, suffering from original sin. In this regard, Taylor Stoehr has written that "Darnay's guilt appears to be hereditary." Albert Hutter and Law-rence Frank, moreover, in articles previously cited, have both argued convincingly that he is guilty also of a kind of parricide, having imagined or willed the death of his father's twin brother, the evil Marquis, just hours or perhaps minutes before the latter's murder. But one does not need a Christian or a Freudian interpretation to under-stand the guilt feelings of a man who was told by his mother when he was two years old that unless he can find and reconcile the needle-in-a-haystack sister of the peasant girl his father had wronged, "atonement would one day be required of him." Moreover, guilt is a specialty of the romantic hero in Dickens's later novels.

In the essays he wrote about the Pantomime at various points in his career, Dickens had interesting things to say about most of the figures, but Harlequin was described only as an ordinary man "to be found in no particular walk or degree, on whom a certain station, or particular conjunction of circumstances, confers the magic wand." In other words, he is lucky enough to be loved by Columbine, and this luck seems to be the one most significant aspect of the character Dickens derived from Harlequin. Two years after the publication of the essay in question, when he was driving towards the conclusion of *Nicholas Nickleby* and setting up what I believe to be the first panto-mime within his fiction, Dickens had pantaloon-wearing Ralph Nickleby say of his Harlequin nephew, "There is some spell about that boy. . . . Circumstances conspire to help him. Talk of fortune's favours! What is even money to such Devil's luck as this?" Thus began, if it did not begin even earlier in *Oliver Twist,* a line of Dickens heroes who narrowly escape death in war or by plague or shipwreck or attempted murder or who are selected arbitrarily to become gentlemen, while the Uriah Heeps and Orlicks eat their hearts out. In *The Frozen Deep,* the Wilkie Collins–Charles Dickens play which inspired the writing of *A Tale of Two Cities,* Richard Wardour, the model for Sydney Carton, says contemptuously to the man whom he has not yet recognized as his rival but for whom he will ultimately sacrifice his own life, "You have got what the women call a lucky face." And Carton himself regards Charles Darnay similarly when he reflects, "I thought he was rather a handsome fellow, and I thought I should have been much the same sort of fellow if I had had any luck."

Charles is, of course, not only lucky in his face and in love and in his Harlequin knack of always getting out or being gotten out of the deadly scrapes he finds himself in, he is also extremely lucky in his birth as compared to his starving French countrymen. This last mentioned aspect of his luck, moreover, is what relates him most closely to other Dickens heroes and to the guilty feeling heroes in a number of important nineteenth- and twentieth-century novels. Previously, in an article called "Faulkner's Isaac and the American Ishmael," I dealt with a recurring relationship in American fiction between one man, who has inherited because he was lucky enough to have been born white, and his disinherited brother, no less a man than he, but of a different race. The biblical story this relationship was always intended to bring to mind was, of course, that of the young Ishmael, who was cast out into the wilderness, deprived both of material prosperity and of his share in the Covenant because he was replaced by his younger brother Isaac, who had the luck to be born legitimate. I was especially interested in the fact that American writers, not only Melville and Faulkner, but, of course, Cooper, Hawthorne, Stowe, Twain and others were not so much interested in depicting the anguish of the rejected Ishmael as they were in showing the guilt of the reluctantly inheriting Isaac. In British fiction and especially in the novels of Dickens, as I was later on to see, this relationship is not between individuals of different races but of different economic classes. In America a white Isaac feels uneasy with the thought that the plantation he has inherited should really have gone to his black brother Ishmael; in Dickens, from as early as *Oliver Twist,* a gentleman feels guilty or should feel guilty with the thought that he is living on a patrimony to which he has no legitimate right so long as others of his species are impoverished. Nicholas Nickleby and Smike are very much like an interracial pair out of American literature.

From very early in his career, from at least as early as *Martin Chuzzlewit,* Dickens tended to combine the luck of his Harlequin figures, the romantic lovers, with feelings of guilt. Walter Gay, who plays this role in *Dombey and Son,* was originally intended to be corrupted by the business morality of the novel's world and the Dick Whittington—sell-your-best-friend-and-rise-in-the-world—dreams of his friends. David Copperfield, the hero of the novel which bears his name, is so troubled by vague and undefinable guilt feelings—about his friend's seduction of Little Em'ly, about the early death of the wife he had grown tired of, about his dealings with the servant class from which he sprung, about his own rise in the world—that psychological critics have recently been having a field day with him, converting what used to be regarded in Chesteronian days as the blandest of Dickens's characters into one of the most complex. Arthur Clennam, the middle-aged, dreary, romantic lover of *Little Dorrit,* who instead of marrying his sweetheart allowed himself to be shipped off to China, returns with a crippling sense of unworthiness and with a guilty suspicion that the capital on which he lives must have been stolen from someone else. And since Arthur can't find anyone with a legitimate claim on his money and cannot put his finger on any crime he has actually committed, he manages both to impoverish himself and to find himself guilty by investing his own and his partner's funds in a fraudulent financial scheme which goes bankrupt. He fairly rejoices at having done something worthy of being put into prison for.

Pip, the romantic hero of the novel which follows *A Tale of Two Cities,* is similarly successful in getting rid of the shame he has been made to feel in his youth by parlaying it into real guilt, guilt at having snobbishly rejected the people who are dearest to him, and especially at not having rejected the destructive metaphor current in the novel which divides humanity into genteel predators—hounds or spiders— and impoverished victims—varmints or insects—instead of acknowledging everyone, as Joe Gargery does, as a fellow creature. Pip is, of course, both the luckiest and the guiltiest of the romantic heroes, lucky enough to get a fortune merely by wishing for it, and so guilty that Dickens could not make up his mind in the first draft of the novel to let him marry the heroine.

On the other hand, Charles Darnay does most emphatically get the girl, although, as we have seen, she is virtually the only character in *A Tale of Two Cities,* including himself, who can stand him. Charles's marriage, in fact, occurs in the sixteenth of the thirty-one serial parts of the novel, that is to say, the very center, always the place of highest significance in a Dickens story. "Charles Darnay's way," we are told by the author, is the one way "the world of man has invariably gone . . . the way of the love of a woman." He is so lucky that even the immense power of his sense of guilt and unworthiness has no ultimate force against him.

Nevertheless, we ought not to underestimate the depth of that sense of guilt, and we should, I think, give due attention to the question of how far it is justified in relation to the principal action and historical event of *A Tale of Two Cities*: the French Revolution; that is to say, how much of Charles Darnay's guilt is not only an expression of the condition of man after the Fall and of undeniable psychological trauma, but is caused and perhaps justified by Charles's failures as social man.

To begin with, he has not fulfilled the first charge of his life, to sell his mother's jewels and give the money to the sister of the raped peasant girl, Madame Defarge, as it turns out. In fact, we are not told that Charles so much as made an attempt at carrying out this obligation, although it is possible that this is what he was trying to do on those mysterious trips between England and France between 1775 and 1780. This is special pleading in Charles's behalf, for there is no evidence, but I can think of no other explanation for the secrecy of these journeys, a secrecy which, at his English trial for treason, Charles maintains at very serious expense to his case and danger to his life. He told Lucie he "was travelling under an assumed name" because he "was travelling on a business of a delicate and difficult nature, which might get people into trouble." He could not have been divesting himself of his estate, for he had not come into that yet, and it is difficult to imagine who, besides himself and anti-aristocratic agents helping in the search for the wronged girl, might be in any danger. Still it is curious that *Dickens* maintains the secrecy, and curious also that Darnay, usually so apt to feel guilty, does not torture himself about this failure to carry out his mother's first command.

On the other hand, Darnay is distraught at his powerlessness to, as he says, "execute the last request of my dear mother's lips, and obey the last look of my dear mother's eyes, which implored me to have mercy and to redress." The powerlessness comes, presumably, from Charles's situation of having been passed over in the inheritance—his wicked uncle rules instead of him—but when he does succeed to the estate, just hours after making this speech, he is still unable to perform effectively:

> he had acted imperfectly. He knew very well, that in his love for Lucie, his renunciation of his social place, though by no means new to his mind, had been hurried and incomplete. He knew that he ought to have systematically worked it out and supervised it, and that he had meant to do it, and that it had never been done. . . . he had watched the times for a time of action . . . until the time had gone by.

But even this confession of failure by Charles misses the point. Presumably his mother's lips and eyes had not implored him to renounce his power, but rather to use it for the sake of the poor.

Nevertheless, the sense of guilt and shame called up by this train of thought impels Charles's return to France for the sake of saving his servant and using his influence to moderate the revolution. Dickens writes "His latent uneasiness had been, that bad aims were being worked out in his own unhappy land by bad instruments, and that he, who could not fail to know that he was better than they, was not there, trying to do something to stay the bloodshed, and assert the claims of mercy and humanity." All very fine, but painful though it is to contradict T. A. Jackson, perhaps the one critic who has something positive to say about Charles, I am not sure Dickens wants us entirely to admire the "large-hearted generosity" of his hero when he sends him back to France, drawn to the loadstone rock. In the first place, he is still not acting to redress as his mother had commanded but only to plead mercy for the members and the agents of his own class. As his assumed name suggests, and it has to be significant in a novel filled with Carlyle's clothing symbols and with symbolic names, Charles Darnay is, at best, a mender, and has no place as part of a revolution. He wants reform; the Defarges, true revolutionaries, want continued abuses to infuriate the people.

In the second place, Charles's impulsive action is strongly reminiscent of the ineffective or unsustained windmill charges on social institutions made by previous romantic heroes in Dickens's novels. He dashes into the French Revolution as Arthur Clennam of *Little Dorrit* took on the Circumlocution Office or as Richard Carstone of *Bleak House* smashed his head against the Court of Chancery. The action is naively vain, as Dickens suggests when he tells us of Darnay that the "glorious vision of doing good, which is so often the sanguine mirage of so many good minds, arose before him, and he even saw himself in the illusion with some influence to guide this raging Revolution." And there is also the possibility of an unworthy subconscious motivation for his action. Since it developed from a sense of shame and guilt, Charles's purpose, like that of Clennam, may be to punish himself. Having failed to redress the wrong as his mother had charged him to do, he may be embracing the opportunity for the violent atonement she had predicted as the alternative. In any event, these are the ways Charles's brief career as a social activist seems destined to turn out— vain and self-destructive.

But before we go too far in joining the chorus which condemns Charles Darnay, it is well to remember that Dickens could never bring himself to believe in the Carlylean hero and that by this time in his career he was highly skeptical of the effectuality of social action of any sort. Dickens may not be criticizing Charles Darnay's qualities as a Revolutionary hero; he is more likely undermining the very concept of romantic heroism by doubting both its motives and its possibilities for success. Charles is at least as powerless in Revolutionary France as he was in bourgeois England, but in the long run he is no less effectual than the other would-be Revolutionary heroes whose fate Carton predicts in the final chapter.

The hero of Bulwer-Lytton's French Revolutionary novel, *Zanoni* (1842), which has long been recognized as one of the sources of *A Tale of Two Cities,* is, unlike Darnay, a figure of immense, almost god-like power in his proper sphere. Nevertheless Zanoni accomplishes nothing to his purpose when he mixes "for the first time . . . among the broils and strategies of man." Zanoni does not altogether fail—he brings about no less an event than the fall of Robespierre—but the purpose for which he acted, which was to save his beloved from the guillotine by hastening the end of the Terror, is absolutely frustrated when Robespierre, foreseeing the end of *his* power, simply advances the date of the execution one day.

> Vain seer [admonishes the author] who wouldst make thyself
> the instrument of the Eternal, the very danger that now best
> the tyrant but expedited the doom of his victims. Tomor-
> row, eighty heads, and her whose pillow has been thy heart.

If the romantic hero cannot find revolutionary identity by acting with romantic, Schilleresque heroism, it is still possible, even in the turmoil of the Revolution, for him to maintain his identity as a lover. Zanoni plays Sydney Carton's part, dying on the guillotine not only for the sake of, but actually in the place of his beloved. And for him it is a significant sacrifice, for having discovered the secret of eternal youth, Zanoni is several hundred years old in 1793 and will live forever if he can only avoid accidents like decapitation.

Similarly, Charles Darnay is rendered physically powerless by the Revolution he had come to France to direct, and he is transformed into a helpless and sleeping infant by the growing strength of Sydney Carton. Nevertheless, he keeps a firm hold on his role as Harlequin. I suggested earlier that the action of the sixteenth number, the wedding of Charles and Lucie, pointed to marriage as the novel's central meaning. Other places one looks for meaning in a Dickens novel are the earliest and latest points of the story. Lawrence Frank notes that "the novel literally and figuratively originates in a rape," and while this is true of work as we have it, in Dickens's earliest manuscript, the younger Evrémonde twin did not rape the peasant girl; he seduced her by pretending to marry her. So the story was intended also to begin with a marriage, albeit a false one. I think *A Tale of Two Cities* ends with a marriage, as well, the marriage of Carton and the little seamstress, whose innocence and occupation identify her as a substitute for Lucie of the golden thread. The three weddings indicate a progress: we begin with a false and secret marriage; move then to the real but strangely private nuptials of Charles and Lucie; and conclude with a wedding which is both symbolic and highly public. This wedding on the scaffold validates Carton and his great sacrifice. He is dying for Darnay and for Darnay's marriage to Lucie. It is perhaps of equal significance that in an unrendered scene of the novel which presumably took place at La Force Prison, Charles Darnay courted Sydney Carton's bride for him. When the girl approaches Sydney and asks if she can hold his hand in the cart, she still mistakes him for his double, whom both he and the reader have neglected to thank, and whose identity, revolutionary and otherwise, is as Harlequin lover.

Death by Water
in *A Tale of Two Cities*

Garrett Stewart

With [a] sense of drowning in *David Copperfield* as a fatality correlative to the narrative activity of the retrospective text that reports it, we are ready for the gradually developed metaphors of death by water in *A Tale of Two Cities* (1859). These figures gather toward and help gloss the sacrificial death of the hero, dispatched of course by the blade and not by drowning, as that death is redeemed in and by narrative. One of the first full-scale renderings of the Parisian scene under the Reign of Terror comes to us filtered through its horrific revelation to the mind of Jarvis Lorry: "All this was seen in a moment, as the vision of a drowning man, or any human creature at any very great pass, could see a world if it were there" (bk. 3, chap. 3). Drowning is Dickens's definitive metaphor for this rite of perceptual passage, with the noun "vision" suspended in the periodic sentence long enough to stand for both effect and cause, vista and empowered eyesight. Fortified by countless later analogies to the Terror as a bloody Flood come again, this simile foresees the visionary acuity that the hero himself achieves when he drowns symbolically in the tidal heave of revolutionary violence.

To place Sydney Carton's sacrifice within this larger historical context, we need to return to the first retributive scene of death in the novel, characterized by Dickens's usual verbal tension and ingenuity. The assassination of the vicious Marquis St. Evrémonde, portrayed as the initiating act of the revolution, leads at the public and private level

From *Death Sentences: Styles of Dying in British Fiction.* © 1984 by the President and Fellows of Harvard College. Harvard University Press, 1984.

directly to the execution of Carton, scapegoat of the Terror. The Marquis is only found dead by narration, not watched die. As in the case of Little Nell, though with an opposite moral implication, the very absence of dramatized transition from life into death is its epitomizing irony. With the Marquis's affectless sly ferocity and his heart of stone, it is only appropriate for prose to discover him unruffled by death, yet already stiffened in its aftermath. The word *death* is never mentioned, but the Gorgon of the ancestral mansion has found "the stone face for which it had waited through about two hundred years" (bk. 2, chap. 9). This face "lay back on the pillow of Monsieur the Marquis. It was like a fine mask, suddenly startled, made angry, and petrified." The Marquis's face never more than a fine mask, the "it" to which it has degenerated is merely the epitomizing gist of its living nature, rigidified from within, until now, not by fear but by callousness. The final word in that serial syntax replaying the murder thus negotiates by ambiguity another familiar Dickensian interval (here only by retrospect and implication) between vanishing life and finality. The idiomatic reading of "petrified" in which an extremity of feeling would bring on a catalepsy of terror, a normative human reaction in the face of this sudden mortal violence, seems immediately absorbed into and ruled out by the more literal understanding of the term. The moral rigor mortis of the aristocracy is thus prolonged uninterruptedly into death from a life of chilling hauteur. The ultimate stylistic effect achieved by the reiterated severance of the "it"—stony face detached from stabbed torso—is to offer up the Marquis, as inaugural victim of the Terror, to that epidemic of decapitation that will be rife in the land with the coming of la Guillotine.

Rage swollen to the breaking point, the floodgates of bloodshed are now thrown open. This figurative sense of the nightmare to follow is no dead metaphor in the novel. Murderous impulse is repeatedly imagined as the impetus of inundation—as in those rivers of blood for which that broken wine cask in the famous fifth chapter is a prototype. The carnage grows intoxicating and inexorable. With the return of the Marquis to a stone-cold gargoyle in the dead edifice of his world, Dickens begins the transformation from historical time into apocalyptic time, the fixating of the former with moribund stasis along with the release of the latter into a set of images derived from the Flood in Genesis. This is the ultimate manner, too, in which this first dramatic death scene in the novel is channeled directly into, and filtered clean by, the sacrificial (and literal) decapitation of the hero, Carton, where the apocalyptic images of flood that follow from the Marquis's murder are internalized as the private mind's "drowning" vision. It is a vision compressed and, in the hero's access to narrative grace, prophetic.

In a novel that drops in passing an apocalyptic hint about the Day of Judgment when the "ocean is . . . to give up its dead" (bk. 2, chap. 2), the explicit imagery of flood and drowning begins innocuously enough as a double turn of phrase in that very chapter, "The Wine-Shop," that gives us in symbol the first overspill of revolutionary desperation. The underprovided lamps of the Saint Antoine quarter are seen there to provide merely "dim wicks" that "swung in a sickly manner overhead, as if they were at sea" (bk. 1, chap. 5). The simile is then shifted over to idiom and to omen: "Indeed they were at sea, and the ship and crew were in peril of tempest." From that point on the metaphor rarely lets up. Building toward the outbreak of violence, one chapter closes in an eightfold paratactic spate of clauses begun with the rush of literal water and sped quickly to metaphor: "The water of the fountain ran, the swift river ran, the day ran into evening, so much life in the city ran into death according to rule, time and tide waited for no man," and so on as "all things ran their course" (bk. 2, chap. 7). It is not long before the "living sea" of mob violence "rose, wave on wave, depth on depth," a vast and "resistless . . . ocean" (bk. 2, chap. 21). The irreversible momentum of this flood runs straight into the title of the subsequent chapter, "The Sea Still Rises," and from there into the third book, where the "current" of death continues to "rend" and "strew" (bk. 3, chap. 6) its victims.

By this third book, however, the figures are undergoing a certain internalization as well, so that Darnay in prison, hearing the distant "swell that rose" against him, also finds "scraps tossing and rolling upward from the depth of his mind" (bk. 3, chap. 1). His double, Carton, tending to his own life as a merely troubled, restless, superficial swirl in the torrent of history, is more ironically self-conscious about the application of tidal analogies before an actual river: "The strong tide, so swift, so deep, and certain, was like a congenial friend" in which he sees glassed a replica of his own relation to it, "watching an eddy that turned and turned purposeless, until the stream absorbed it, and carried it on to the sea.—Like me!" (bk. 3, chap. 9). Just before that self-accusatory internal echo ("sea" / "me"), Carton's "chain" of reverie leads him back to thoughts of his father's funeral, retrieving its recited sacred text "like a rusty old ship's anchor from the deep." The tacit idiom "chain of association" is thus aptly literalized as the recovery of a previous being far submerged in the internal tides of mind. For this man who had once characterized himself to Lucie Manette as "like one who died young" (bk. 2, chap. 13), the memory of his father's funeral is a partial resurrection of his earlier self coincident with the now recalled words, "I am the Resurrection and the Life." A confession of Carton's previous psychic burial is cannily unlocked in this same paragraph within the most straightforward of idioms: "Long ago, when he had been famous among his earliest competitors as a youth of great promise, he had *followed his father to the grave*. His mother had died, years before (my emphasis on Dickens's funereal duplicity). In a single phrase we find the justification for all that macabre comedy about grave robbing that centers around Jerry Cruncher as Resurrection Man. It is Carton, not only orphaned but interred, who must be "recalled to life" again in a lifting out of himself that raises him to the sacrificial scaffold, regardless of any further elevation by death itself.

Lazarus-like, making good on the first person of the Lord's annunciation, Carton ascends not through but to his death scene, from the stilled "deep" of his humanity into that public storm where "fifty-two were to roll that afternoon on the life-tide of the city to the boundless everlasting sea" (bk. 3, chap. 13). Even the figurative verb there is a threefold pun compounding the oceanic metaphor of death with its literal cause and effect in the remorseless roll of the condemned and the consequent roll of their heads under the guillotine. For the man whose mother had died in his infancy, his goal, shared with the seamstress whom he has befriended in his last hours, will be to rejoin the "Universal Mother" across the untraversable distance of death's "dark highway." It is a distance implicated in the interval of a nearby play on words, Carton and the girl hoping "to repair home together, and to rest in her bosom" (bk. 3, chap. 15), where the imagined journey to their long home overtakes and includes the sense of a "reparation" for all earthly losses.

There, as throughout the death scene, the violent revolutionary sea changes seem to set in motion a compensatory verbal rhythm of wavering and restitution. As Carton nears his and the book's end, the Dickensian rhetoric detaches crucial phrases from within, releases words to each other in new ways, submits the burden of the unsayable to the ebb and turn of surprising allusions, nuances, and ambiguities. Here is the death of the seamstress just before Carton: "She goes next before him—is gone; the knitting-women count Twenty-Two" (bk. 3, chap. 15). A semicolon keeps separate the ledger of vendetta—ticking off its corpses with mindless metronomic precision—from the empathetic prose of the dying, clocked to a more humane rhythm. Across the dash of the scaffold's inflexible continuity in numeration and its fatal haitus, the verb of motion, "goes," becomes the past participle of absence in "is gone," a phrase inserted above the line in Dickens's manuscript as a masterly afterthought. Similarly the adverb "next" and the preposition "before," each not only spatial but temporal, are evaporated with temporality itself into the paradoxical present tense of instantaneous removal, "is gone," predicting still what in the same interval it eradicates. Imagine the phrase otherwise and you hear what Dickensian tact has managed with the grammatical parataxis, "She goes next before him and is gone." With the refusal of ordinary conjunction in the world's terms, the suspended tense of "is" lingers across the split second of recorded absence as a softening consecration of the girl's impress, if not still her presence, for the man who came out of himself to care.

That phrase "next before him" is the last direct reference, even by pronoun, to the hero. After a paragraph reiterating the text of "I am the Resurrection and the Life," we pass to another elided interval: "The murmuring of many voices, the upturning of many faces, the pressing on of many footsteps in the outskirts of the crowd, so that it swells forward in a mass like one great heave of water, all flashes away. Twenty-Three." In that long periodic building toward recapitulated subject and burst verb for the death sentence, the final predication of the hostile mob at its falling away from the hero, his from it, compresses its gerundive forms, the named actions of the inimical world in all its otherness, weight, and forward thrust, lets its grammar heap forward even into a suspensive independent clause ("so that it swells"), and then, at the pivotal instant of similitude (the monosyllabic massing at "like one great heave of water") undercuts the whole cumulative grammar of the world's inertial resistance with a dismissive idiom. The phrase "flashes away" is not only a formulaic description of drowning quite common in literary treatments, a description enforced by the explicit analogy to the heaving furrows of "water"—but it is also an echo of that earlier murder of Madame Defarge and the sacrificial impairment of Miss Pross: " 'I feel,' said Miss Pross, 'as if there had been a flash and a crash, and that crash was the last thing I should ever hear in this life' " (bk. 3, chap. 14). Locution there for an explosive burst of light, "flash" has gone from noun of ignition to a verb of extinguishment across a pattern of mortal displacement captured by Dickensian prose at the level of echoing monosyllables. For what Miss Pross, clinging to Madame Defarge "with more than the hold of a drowning woman," saw and heard, the murderousness of the world turned against itself, is what Carton will no longer be made to suffer, having taken the violence unto himself as his own liberating fate. The canceling "crash" that follows the earlier gunpowder "flash" has become the guillotine's twice-repeated "Crash!" by which the whole scene of terror, in a chiastic inversion of the earlier death scene and its rhetoric, is finally "flashed" away for Carton, at the moment when the ferocious ocean of hate both overtakes and cleanses him.

I invoke the notion of a purging inundation advisedly, for the executioner's "Number Twenty-Three"—in its mindless recoil from subjective to objective reality—is a terminal code for the name in which this death by symbolic drowning does in fact miraculously, if at one level deceptively, baptise Carton: the name of the man Darnay for whom he dies. This is, we may remember, the novel of so deft a liturgical wit that its comic denomination of Jerry Cruncher is referred back to baptism as "the youthful occasion of his renouncing by proxy the works of darkness" (bk. 2, chap. 1). So does Carton endure his more extreme renunciation as a proxy for his double and recent namesake. When the revolutionary violence, in its focal reception by Jarvis Lorry, is earlier compared to the "vision" of the drowning mind, that perception is described as empowering the synoptic access to an entire world "if it were there" (bk. 3, chap. 3). The "world" that Carton's later figurative incarnation of a "drowning man" might now envision "if it were there" is the world that, through his death, is brought into being—the world of the future that his doom ensures for the family whose safety he dies to make possible. At this "pass of a crisis," as that explicit earlier conceit of drowning had it—this mortal impasse and passing on—retrospect is replaced by prophecy for a man who has no past worth looking back on, only another's future worth dying for.

What follows is a typical Dickensian survey of the future fortunes of his cast internalized as if it were the "sublime and prophetic" insight of his dying hero. Yet his visionary coda retains also its aura of a textual prototype, as we will see, the moment of death discovered virtually to novelize its own succession in the vanishing interval of last consciousness. When Carton tells Lucy earlier in the novel, "I am like one who died young," he adds, "All my life might have been" (bk. 2, chap. 13). Indeed, Darnay is the living embodiment of what he might have been: alter ego of Carton's emotional desuetude in life, projected continuation of his identity across the defied severance of death. With any meaningful past only faintly conjectural, Carton has at least in death earned the right to have his legacy appear before him with the strange declarative certainty of the (the paradox seems inescapable) prophetically remembered. This unprecedented shift in perspective, in the distended interval annulled consciousness, is the ultimate metastasis or "remove" of mortal transition in Dickens: the instantaneous break from time redirected into an unbroken futurity rhetorically set forth.

These last five paragraphs of the book, inscribed for us as if they had been transcribed by Carton, gain a portion of their force by falling in line with other deathbed narratives in the novel and their summarizing truth. Darnay, after all, is sentenced, Carton executed in his stead, because of the incriminating narrative document scribbled with his last strength by Dr. Manette in the Bastille during what he thought were his final days alive. This is a narrative of aristocratic cruelty for which the chief evidence, besides the doctor's incarceration itself, is his own transcription within it of another deathbed narrative, orally delivered, of the young man whose family was destroyed by the cruelty of the Evrémondes. Carton's hypothetical last words thus shift the emphasis of such nested tragic reports forward into a purgative futurity, delivered up into our narrative as if Carton had been handed quill and paper on the scaffold. Indeed we hear of the "remarkable" woman executed shortly before him who was "allowed to write down the thoughts that were inspiring her," thoughts authorized by finality, intensified by death. "If we had given an utterance to his, and they were prophetic, they would have been these" (bk. 3, chap. 15). Dickens drops out the second and expected "if" under cover of parallelism, so that these thoughts are in fact predicated and deemed prophetic apart from any mystery that might be thought to cloak them for want of transcription. Insinuated with the impunity of ellipsis, they *were* prophetic, written or not.

There is a further inside-out turn to this narrative involution at the close. That manuscript of accusation against the house of Evrémonde was not the only narrative composed by Doctor Manette in prison, nor the only one binding the far future to the present implications of a tale. Besides this political injunction to retributive murder, Manette was also a prophetic narrator of domestic eventualities, jotting down in his mind, not on paper, alternative scenarios for the future life of the child he never saw born. One of these unwritten mental fictions is a remarkable negative anticipation of the novel's own metanarrative close. On the eve of her marriage to Charles, Manette confesses to Lucie how in his worst prison fantasy he had imagined his own oblivion in his daughter's eyes. He uses the same parallel grammar as in Carton's multiple "I see's" at the end, pushing his reiterations forward to a just barely suppressed metaphor of texuality: "I have pictured my daughter, to myself, as perfectly forgetful of me," he recalls. "I have cast up the years of her age . . . I have seen her married . . . I have altogether perished from the remembrance of the living, and in the next generation my place was a blank" (bk. 2, chap. 17). It is this blank—not just emptiness but ellipsis, not just oblivion but textual hiatus in the imagined book of record—that death permits the redemptive hero to inscribe with better meaning, both for himself and for the descendants of Manette.

We are now ready to watch Carton watching—and tracing out for himself in a mental inscription—the very future precipitated by his present-tense sacrifice from the otherwise effacing flow of time. Early in the novel, anticipating the "I see" pattern at the close, Carton "saw for a moment . . . a mirage of honorable ambition, self-denial, and perseverance." The paradisal "fair city of this vision," with "airy galleries from which the loves and graces looked upon him" (bk. 2, chap. 5), is to be replaced by a fatal sacrifice of undreamed "self-denial" that sends forth identity not into some heavenly city of purpose but into the secular "perserverance" of history itself. The closural pattern of rhythmic repetition is one that Dickens visibly labored over at the manuscript stage, subdividing an already drafted clause at one point so as, by introducing more "I see's," to promote the momentum of this visionary anaphora. The metaphors of rising and resurrection are first contrasted—"I see Barsad, and Cly, Defarge, The Vengeance, the Jury-man, the Judge, long ranks of the new oppressors who *have risen* on the destruction of the old, perishing by this retributive instrument" —until the flood subsides and brotherhood reasserts itself: "I see a beautiful city and a brilliant people *rising* from this abyss" (my stress on the shift from preterite to prophetic participle). The next paragraph opens, "I see the lives for which I lay down my life, peaceful, useful, prosperous and happy, in that England which I shall see no more," where the ambiguous quartet of congratulatory adjectives could apply grammatically to Carton's own passing "life" as well in his moment of recaptured purpose. "I see Her with a child upon her bosom . . . I see the old man . . . passing tranquilly to his reward." Carton's vision then presses on from this future death scene into the next paragraph, where the conjugal embrace of Lucie and Charles is epitomized in their final closeness underground: "I see her and her husband, their course done, lying side by side in their last earthly bed . . . I see that child who lay upon her bosom and bore my name . . . foremost of just judges and honoured men, bringing a boy of my name . . . to this place—then fair to look upon" (like the "fair city" of his early "mirage"). In this way the present apocalyptic judgment extends, softened, into the inherited vocation that Carton as law clerk could never muster in his own person.

Enunciated in the unvoiced cadences of sublime confidence, style thus humanizes into visionary view the last interval of a death scene. The ordinary agnosticism of Dickensian dying, its end-stopped character, the opacity of its high finish—all is qualified by the flavor of augury, but not, in the other sense, of divination. Degenerated history, exploded toward revolution and apocalypse by the death of Marquis St. Evrémonde, is returned after the flood of bitter judgment into the flow of temporal history again, regenerate now, imaginable by narrative even in its merely eventual shapes. The frequent superimposition of narrated drowning and fictional self-consciousness, in their common penchant for retrospective order and summation, is layered yet further with this access to the future as a virtually narrative feat, almost as if the hero had "been allowed to write down" his consolatory thoughts after all. These thoughts are couched like all fiction in the self-confirming authority of pure invention. What rumor assures us—the rehearsal of life in drowning—here becomes in the other sense of preview or try-out the only real life there is for the hero to rehearse. Yet two things must be kept in mind so as to clarify the nature of this coda. First, Carton does not see into and through the grave of his own fate to some intimation of immortality, or at least not until the novel's last clause. From the edge of eternity he peers back into the world of time, and forward there, as if through eternity's sanction as an incomparable vantage on time, into confident earthly prefiguration. Second, it is the final decorum of the novel as record, however fictional, that the generations availed and so evoked by Carton's sacrifice do not outdistance the time elapsed between the Revolution and Dickens's writing of the novel in the middle of the next century. Even within the myth of clairvoyance the authority of fiction, like the authority of deathbed revelation, is held to the precincts of retrospect.

To assert further the connection between novel making and this visionary dispensation, all Carton's prophetic seeing closes down at the

end upon an overheard story, the hero imagining Lucie's son narrating
for her grandson, Sydney's namesake, the whole narrative of his life up
to and including his death: "And I hear him tell the child my story, with
a tender and faltering voice." It is as if the dying Hamlet were shown
overhearing in is own mind's ear the explanatory oration he has
ordered of Horatio. In the vanishing interval of final consciousness,
Carton's metaphorically drowning mind does indeed look back on the
story of his soul's dark night told over as conscious tragic narrative, a
story of course transfigured by the death that offers it up as completed
and transmissible tale. No novel could fasten more surely the always
tacit bond between mortality and communicable narration. Carton's
dramatized and consummating death scene is displaced into an articulate exemplum discovered at the very moment of his death to be
recoverable in the telling, time out of mind. And so the tale recounted
by Lucie's son becomes, in short—and of course in its shortened
form—the title scene of the *Tale* that earns its closure by foreseeing it.

This metanarrative redoubling then gives way to the last sentence,
comprising the last paragraph, of the novel, perhaps the most famous
brief soliloquy in all of Dickens. It arrives as if to instance in abbrevi-
ated form the very "story" of Carton's life, summation in light of
peripety and redemption, and to understand this story as precisely the
province of last utterance, unvoiced or not: "It is a far, far better thing
that I do, than I have ever done; it is a far, far better rest that I go to
than I have ever known." Death emerges here as both heroic action
and its reward, moral resolve and at the same time temporal resolution, the valiant doing and the having done with. It is at the core of
their power that these lines do not vie with the novel's opening
sentence as the most famous in Dickens but seem to eventuate from
within that anarchic parataxis desperately struggling for containment
by antithesis. In the initiating chapter called, with apocalyptic overtones of premature closure in a time out of joint, "The Period,"
we have heard, "It was the best of times, it was the worst of times, it
was the age of wisdom, it was the age of foolishness," and so forth,
back and forth toward chaos. What is so unforgettable about the
novel's finishing pair of contrastive clauses is that they take up, work
over, and reconstitute this paradoxical deadlock at the outset. There
hyperbole is pitted against hyperbole in a specter of historical contradiction collapsed inward upon itself, imploded and immobilized. Any
curative rhetoric must require a meliorating breadth between extremi-

ties sufficient to declare a direction. From the self-conscious barrage of the first weighted and heightened sentence, which boasts "the superlative degree of comparison only" (that phrasing itself almost a logical paradox), the novel must make its way toward the freed-up incremental style of the true comparative degree in "far, far better," twice repeated at the end in a triumph not over the previous worse or worst so much as over the historical ultimacy when acme and abjection are at one, where time itself as principle of movement and differentiation is fused shut in the insistent plural "times." The hero's communion with pure futurity at the end, when it turns him to the equal purity of completion and retrospect in the last sentence, is thus cadenced in a rectifying echo of the novel's opening. Deep within the rhetoric that attends the communal or fraternal sacrifice of a single life is found the attempted vindication of an epoch.

It happens that the last two pairs of antithetical statements strung on that pendulous syntax of the opening sentence—"we had everything before us, we had nothing before us, we were all going direct to Heaven, we were all going direct the other way"—describe nothing so much as a societal death scene under the aspect first of religion versus atheism, fronting on eternity or void, and then of the two alternatives within a Christian faith, heaven or hell. These simplistic, conflicting overstatements must all be moderated and remade by the rhythm of the novel's last sentence and the waiting ambivalence of its last word. However much the final sentence is designed in obliquely tunneled allusion to the book's opening, its chaos of contradiction now sorted to order, still it allows a final interval within a single verb that also makes it one last instance of immediacy phased forward into the advent of recognized rest and backward into retrospect. The novel's last word is the conduit of a kind of vocabular grace, acknowledging a peace perhaps blessed as well as merely absolute. The rest I take here and now, says (or thinks) Carton to himself, is better, because more complete, than any I have before *taken*; the rest I now set forth upon will not only be better than any I have ever had, but better than I have ever, in my spiritual doubts, known *it would or could be*. On the second understanding of "known" to mean conceptual rather than empirical knowledge, that fretless preknowing of belief, the phrase edges past fact into an elliptical expression of achieved faith, an expression elusively revealed in the very language that reiterates its lifelong absence.

The uncertain valence of "known" thus widens the final grammar only so as to draw it closed again across the semantic interval—a postponed model of death's own instantaneous shift of register—between a past prescience unfelt and an impending nescience momentarily reimagined as ecstatic stasis. Within the vigilant options of its own possibilities in this very last word of the novel, style has once more, and in more senses than one, seen a character through. From "all flashes away" in the actual subjective death sentence, across the period and textual break (suspension as well as severance) at "Number Twenty-Three," the phenomenal passes to the brutally numerical, while at the same time displacing the numenal forward into this whole last monologue. It is a mortal vision which, in its own verbal suspension, would seem to have reinhabited, or even to have broken from and outlasted, the very interval of evacuated consciousness at death.

Close study of Carton's death scene and its visionary coda should have made clear that the extended passage could scarcely have been conceived as the straightforward hallmark of Victorian moral fanfare and uplift, of pathos, threnody, and catharsis, in the guise of which it has passed into literary and popular history. It is not just an exercise in but an exploration of the style of dying as a narrative act, the clefts of its alert and crafted prose activated across narrative time to suggest the evanescent momentum of traversed intervals. It is also a study in the rhetorical power as well as the verbal implementation of death in narrative. Any such sense that the execution of Carton is not only enrolled on the rosters of vengeance but inscribed self-consciously in a novel, a rhetorically motivated sacrifice we as readers somehow demand, takes us back to the first chapter of real plot after the introductory vantage on the times, a plot that knows itself as plot, for Mr. Lorry is repeatedly described there, with a pun on mail-coach ticketing, as the "passenger booked by this history" (bk. 1, chap. 2). So is Carton "booked," first to be resurrected from his own past and then to be preserved by "this history" of Dickens. He dies so as to secure the shape of this history for others coming, which of course means only for us, even "generations hence."

In an accompanying turn of rhetorical bravura, Dickens indicates Carton's sacrificial role as suffering stand-in for the readers as well as for his private double and the Darnay circle. Immediately after Carton admits to the young seamstress that he is in fact "dying for him" (bk. 3, chap. 13), for the man she previously saw in his place—and shortly before the fatal blank at "all flashes away"—there is an earlier break in the text and an unsettling shift into first-person plural. We are suddenly catapulted into the scene of escape, deposited in the same carriage that rushes Darnay, Lucie, and the rest from Paris in a reversal of the coach journey toward France that began the plot. This time we too, in the double sense, are "booked by this history," so that it is we for whom the hero has acknowledged his sacrifice, we who benefit (through a melodramatic shift in pronouns) from the dispensation of displacement. As the chapter closes after paragraphs of frenetic first person, "the whole wild night is in pursuit of us; but, so far, we are pursued by nothing else." We are haunted only by the atmosphere of the novel we are reading, our imaginations alone taking "flight."

At this turn it is essential to recognize that such a narrative foregrounding of sacrificial death, its redemption in and through reading, has nothing to do with aestheticized dying. Dickens is shortly to satirize just this with those "riders in the tumbrils" who choose to "cast upon the multitude such glances as they have seen in theatres, and in pictures" (bk. 3, chap. 15)—or, presumably, such as they have read about in novels. Avoiding this prettified good death, Carton's end, and the structural mechanics of chronology that lock it into place, provide a representational sacrifice for the engaged reader. Guided by that elaborate rhetoric of transposition that eases Carton toward and over the threshold of his dying, the hero's epitomizing end as Ressurrection Man is then displaced into narrative prophecy, as we have seen, and made available there far into the future. The auspicious narrative the hero might have written down if he could have is the predictive story the narrator tells for him under the auspices of omniscience, closing (in on itself) as it does with a future hearing of the novel's own abridged *Tale* lived through to its point of meaning in selfless martyrdom. In this conversion of life line to story line, we realize that the imagery of drowning may well appear at the instant of Carton's death as a popular equivalent to the fictional self-involvement of Dickens's closure. Summoned here is the paradigm of mortal replay, which suggests that time is not abrogated by death so much as gathered up one time, life brought to shape as it is brought to a close, whether in a flash of memory or as a function of record.

Even before this, it is our own relation to the whole record of death that has been dramatized by that striking transition into first-person present tense. Rhetoric in recognition of its own service, the passage is designed to reorient us as fellow travelers with the Darnay party, "pursued" as "we are" from the scene of tragedy into the open-ended world of its true comprehension. Fictional death by proxy translates to a displacement of fatality for the reader as well as Darnay. *A Tale of Two Cities* thereby nears its close with not only a demonstration but also a parable of the fictional death sentence and its resonance, acknowledging those "booked" heroes who die for us at the arm's length of aesthetic distance. When history, made present to us on that road out of Paris by the shifting grammar of tense, further includes us by the encompassing grammar of number, Dickens has more self-consciously than in any other of his novels inscribed that narrative place, the safe and sometimes curative space, of fictional substitution and catharsis—the dying that is far, far better in art.

Dickens and the Catastrophic Continuum of History in *A Tale of Two Cities*

J. M. Rignall

It is not surprising that the most remembered scene in *A Tale of Two Cities* is the last, for this novel is dominated, even haunted, by its ending. From the opening chapter in which the "creatures of this chronicle" are set in motion "along the roads that lay before them," while the Woodman Fate and the Farmer Death go silently about their ominous work, those roads lead with sinister inevitability to the revolutionary scaffold. To an unusual extent, especially given the expansive and centrifugal nature of Dickens's imagination, this is an end-determined narrative whose individual elements are ordered by an ending which is both their goal and, in a sense, their source. In a historical novel like this there is a transparent relationship between narrative form and historical vision, and the formal features of *A Tale*—its emphatic linearity, continuity, and negative teleology—define a distinctive vision of history. As Robert Alter has argued in his fine critical account of the novel, it is not the particular historical event that ultimately concerns Dickens here, but rather a wider view of history and the historical process. That process is a peculiarly grim one. As oppression is shown to breed oppression, violence to beget violence, evil to provoke evil, a pattern emerges that is too deterministic to owe much to Carlyle and profoundly at odds with the conventional complacencies of Whig history. Instead of progress there is something more like the catastrophic continuum that is Walter Benjamin's description of the historical process: the single catastrophe, piling wreckage upon wreckage.

From *ELH* 51, no. 3 (Fall 1984). © 1984 by the Johns Hopkins University, Baltimore/London.

And when, in the sentimental postscript of Carton's prophecy, Dickens finally attempts to envisage a liberation from this catastrophic process, he can only do so, like Benjamin, in eschatological terms. For Benjamin it was the messianic intervention of a proletarian revolution that would bring time to a standstill and blast open the continuum of history; for Dickens it is the Christ-like intervention of a self-sacrificing individual that is the vehicle for a vision of a better world which seems to lie beyond time and history. The parallel with Benjamin cannot be pressed beyond the common perception of a pernicious historical continuum and the common desire to break it, but the coexistence of these two elements in *A Tale* is, I wish to argue, important for an understanding of the novel, lending it a peculiarly haunted and contradictory quality as Dickens gives expression to a vision of history which both compels and repels him at the same time.

In Carton's final vision of a world seemingly beyond time, the paradigm of the apocalypse mediates between what is known of history and what may be hoped for it. That hope is not to be dismissed as mere sentimentality, whatever the manner of its expression. However inadequately realized Carton's prophecy may be in imaginative terms, it is significant as a moment of resistance to the grimly terminal linearity and historical determinism of the preceding narrative. That resistance is not confined to the last page of the novel, for, as I shall show, it manifests itself in other places and in other ways, creating a faint but discernible counter-current to the main thrust of the narrative. This is not to say that Dickens presents a thorough-going deconstruction of his own narrative procedures and version of history in *A Tale,* for the process at work here is more ambiguous and tentative than that. There is a struggle with sombre fears that gives rise to contradictions which cannot be reduced to the internal self-contradictions of language. What the novel presents is, rather, the spectacle of an imagination both seized by a compelling vision of history as a chain of violence, a catastrophic continuum, and impelled to resist that vision in the very act of articulation, so that the narrative seems at the same time to seek and to shun the violent finality of its ending in the Terror. The nightmare vision is too grim to accept without protest, and too powerful to be dispelled by simple hopefulness, and the work bears the signs of this unresolved and unresolvable contradiction.

In his preface Dickens maintains that the idea of the novel had "complete possession" of him, and the state of imaginative obsession in which *A Tale of Two Cities* was written can be sensed in two rather different aspects of the work: in the way that it presses on relentlessly toward its violent ending, and in the way that particular scenes take on a visionary intensity, seemingly charged with obscure and powerful emotions that are neither fully controlled nor comprehended. The scenes of frenzied collective violence are the most striking examples of this kind of writing, but there are other moments, less obviously related to the main track of the story, when images and ideas erupt into the text with a spontaneous energy that arrests rather than furthers the momentum of the narrative. The first-person meditation on the death-like mystery of individuality which opens chapter 3 ("The Night Shadows") is just such an intervention:

> A wonderful fact to reflect upon, that every human creature is constituted to be that profound secret and mystery to every other. A solemn consideration, when I enter a great city by night, that every one of those darkly clustered houses encloses its own secret; that every room in every one of them encloses its own secret; that every beating heart in the hundreds of thousands of breasts there, is, in some of its imaginings, a secret to the heart nearest it! Something of the awfulness, even of Death itself, is referable to this. No more can I turn the leaves of this dear book that I loved, and vainly hope in time to read it all. No more can I look into the depths of this unfathomable water, wherein, as momentary lights glanced into it, I have had glimpses of buried treasure and other things submerged. It was appointed that the book should shut with a spring, for ever and for ever, when I had read but a page. It was appointed that the water should be locked in an eternal frost, when the light was playing on its surface, and I stood in ignorance on the shore. My friend is dead, my neighbour is dead, my love, the darling of my soul, is dead; it is the inexorable consolidation and perpetuation of the secret that was always in that individuality, and which I shall carry in mine to my life's end. In any of the burial-places of this city through which I pass, is there a sleeper more inscrutable than its busy inhabitants are, in their innermost personality, to me, or than I am to them?

Both the form and the substance of this meditation set it clearly apart from the surrounding narrative. The brooding first-person voice is never heard again in the novel, even though the same sombre note is struck by the impersonal narrator. The directness and urgency of the first-person utterance invite us to look for a significant relationship between these reflections and the main themes of the novel, but it is not easy to find one. The passage is only awkwardly related to the scene on the Dover road which it punctuates, since its insistence on the essential, metaphysical mystery of individuality is out of proportion to the condition of the passengers in the coach. Their mutual suspicion and ignorance are occasioned simply by the hazards of the journey. Nor can it be said to illumine the general condition of life as it appears in this novel. Although there is some connection between the separateness of individuals and the characters and fates of Dr. Manette and Carton, Dickens's handling of character is basically at odds with such an absolute assertion of impenetrable otherness. His imperious command of his characters is never subject to epistemological uncertainty, and even the most estranged figures, like Dr. Manette and Carton, are in the end not mysterious but knowable and known. Except in its tone the excursus is altogether out of place: Dickens here steps out of his own fiction to generalize about character and individuality in life rather than in books, while paradoxically using the metaphor of the book to do so.

This reflection on character and the metaphor that it employs cast a significant light on Dickens's own practice in the novel. By implication, both his presentation of character and his use of an ending are identified as simply matters of literary convention. To see death in terms of the premature closing of a book is to raise the possibility of different relationships among death, narrative, and endings from those presented by *A Tale* itself. Discontinuity is a fact of life and, implicitly, a narrative possibility, and to imply as much is to challenge both the conventional structure of this particular narrative and the vision of historical determinism that it projects. The challenge is only momentary and implied, but the moment is not entirely isolated. Although Dickens primarily uses the death of Carton and the ending of the novel to complete a pattern of meaning rather than to effect a premature closure, there are occasions in the novel when the desire for such a closure surfaces in the text as if in reaction to the chain of violent events that leads relentlessly to the guillotine. The first-person plural dramatization of the Darnays' flight from Paris provides, for instance, a kind of alternative premature ending for those privileged characters who are allowed to escape the logic of the historical process. The scene

is both related and opposed to the "Night Shadows" meditation and
Mr. Lorry's journey to Dover: this time the characters in the coach are
not suspicious, but united by love and shared apprehension; they are
not mysterious and unfathomable, but familiar and transparent. Nevertheless, the "awfulness of death" threatens them from without, and,
as the narrative assumes the urgency and immediacy of the first-person
plural and the present tense, the scene comes to suggest a flight of the
imagination from the foredoomed finality of the guillotine and the
novel's preordained ending. It is a flight which necessarily carries the
characters beyond the boundaries of the novel, which is headed to only
one conclusion, and they never again appear directly in it. Pursued not
by the Revolution but, as it turns out, only by a reflection of their own
fears, they may be said to be escaping from history: "the wind is
rushing after us, and the clouds are flying after us, and the moon is
plunging after us, and the whole wild night is in pursuit of us; but, so
far we are pursued by nothing else." In fleeing the ending of the novel
they have fled beyond the process of history.

There is a less direct and more complex suggestion of flight from
the grim logic of the historical process in the scene of the mob around
the grindstone, observed by Mr. Lorry and Dr. Manette. What they
witness is an appalling spectacle of bestial violence and moral degradation as Dickens lets his wildest and deepest fears rise to the surface.
The chain reaction of violent oppression and violent rebellion has
passed beyond human control, and in this mass frenzy all distinctions
of individuality and even sex are submerged:

> The eye could not detect one creature in the group free from
> the smear of blood. Shouldering one another to get next at
> the sharpening-stone, were men stripped to the waist, with
> the stain all over their limbs and bodies; men in all sorts of
> rags, with the stain upon those rags; men devilishly set off
> with spoils of women's lace and silk and ribbon, with the
> stain dyeing those trifles through and through.

Then, as if appalled by the terrors he has let loose, Dickens, in John
Gross's words, "reaches for his gun":

> And as the frantic wielders of these weapons snatched them
> from the stream of sparks and tore away into the streets, the
> same red hue was red in their frenzied eyes;—eyes which
> any unbrutalised beholder would have given twenty years of
> life, to petrify with a well-directed gun.

> All this was seen in a moment, as the vision of a drowning man, or of any human creature at any very great pass, could see a world if it were there. They drew back from the window, and the Doctor looked for explanation in his friend's ashy face.

Clearly signalled as the vision of a drowning man, the scene is the product of an imagination *in extremis*. It is a bourgeois nightmare of anarchy unleashed by the rebellion of the oppressed. Even if it is the logical culmination of the violent oppression that has preceded it, the violence is, when it eventuates, too great to bear. The "well-directed gun," with its sudden change of focus from dramatic scene to violent, judgmental reaction, looks like an authorial intervention aimed at terminating the nightmare. The curious insistence on the eyes of the frenzied crowd emphasizes that vision is the vital element, and the urge to "petrify" those eyes can be read as the expression of a desire to put an end to that vision. The action is transposed from subject to object: it is not their eyes that Dickens the narrator wishes to close, but his own. For a moment he seeks to retreat from his own vision of the historical process.

There is, then, a form of resistance here to the catastrophic continuum of history, but at the same time Dickens reveals something about the emotional dynamics of that historical process in a way that is more penetrating than the melodramatic simplifications of Madame Defarge and her desire for vengeance. The violent reaction of the "well-directed gun," an answering of violence with violence, implicates the writer himself in the very process he is presenting. This is characteristic of the open and unguarded nature of his procedure in *A Tale*: violent fears and violent reactions are given direct, unmediated expression, so that unwitting parallels emerge between the reflexes of the author/narrator and those of the fictional characters. In this case there is an obvious affinity between the "well-directed gun," with what has been aptly termed its "true ring of outraged rate-paying respectability," and the response of the blustering bourgeois Stryver to news of the Revolution:

> Among the talkers, was Stryver, of the King's Bench Bar, far on his way to state promotion, and, therefore, loud on the theme: broaching to Monseigneur, his devices for blowing the people up and exterminating them from the face of the earth, and doing without them; and for accomplishing

many similar objects akin in their nature to the abolition of eagles by sprinkling salt on the tails of the race.

The reaction of the character is held firmly in focus and identified by means of irony as excessive and senseless, while the author/narrator in the grindstone passage repeats that reaction without the containing frame of any critical awareness. And both reactions have the function— the one deliberate, the other involuntary—of revealing the emotional resources that drive the catastrophic continuum of history. Dickens thus does more than simply project a deterministic vision of history; he shows how that determinism is rooted in commonplace and familiar emotions, how the potential for violence is not confined to a savage past and an alien setting, but lies very close to home. The effect is to detach history from the safety of the past and to suggest that its violent continuum may not have expired with the Revolution.

The persistence of that violence is amply demonstrated by Dickens's own susceptibility to the kinds of powerful emotions that are at work in the novel. As a caricature of the conquering bourgeois, the figure of Stryver belongs as much in the nineteenth century as the eighteenth, and Dickens himself could display distinctly Stryverish leanings in his response to contemporary events. In the same letter to Forster in which he outlines his intentions in *A Tale of Two Cities* and which he must have written about the same time as the grindstone passage, there is a revealing outburst of verbal violence. The letter begins with a discussion of the case of the surgeon Thomas Smethurst, found guilty of poisoning his bigamous "wife." The trial judge, Sir Jonathan Frederick Pollock, strongly supported the verdict in the face of public unease and of moves to persuade the Home Secretary to quash or commute the sentence. Dickens gives his fervent support to Pollock, and in doing so presents another example of an outraged, violent reaction to an act of violence:

> I followed the case with so much interest, and have followed the miserable knaves and asses who have perverted it since, with so much indignation, that I have often had more than half a mind to write and thank the upright judge who tried him. I declare to God that I believe such a service one of the greatest that a man of intellect and courage can render to society. Of course I saw the beast of a prisoner (with my mind's eye) delivering his cut-and-dried speech, and read in every word of it that no one but the murderer could have

delivered or conceived it. Of course I have been driving the girls out of their wits here, by incessantly proclaiming that there needed no medical evidence either way, and that the case was plain without it. Lastly, of course (though a merciful man—because a merciful man I mean), I would hang any Home Secretary (Whig, Tory, Radical, or otherwise) who should step in between that black scoundrel and the gallows.

The protestations of his mercifulness are convincing only as a respectable garment for his Stryverish pugnacity, and the emotional pattern of the passage recapitulates that of the grindstone scene so closely as to provide striking evidence for taking the "well-directed gun" as an authorial intervention. What is more interesting, however, is that the violence spills over into his account of his intentions in writing *A Tale*:

But I set myself the little task of making a *picturesque* story, rising in every chapter with characters true to nature, but whom the story itself should express, more than they should express themselves, by dialogue. I mean, in other words, that I have fancied a story of incident might be written, in place of the bestiality that *is* written under that pretence, pounding the characters out in its own mortar, and beating their own interests out of them. If you could have read the story all at once, I hope you wouldn't have stopped half way.

As violent an exception is taken to conventional forms of storytelling as is taken to an alleged murderer, and when Dickens writes of "pounding" and "beating" his characters it seems that violence is not only central to his vision of history in this novel but is also inherent in his means of expressing that vision. This formal violence, which could be interpreted in one sense as the forcible subordination of character to the story of incident, is as revealingly related to the creation of a narrative and historical continuum as is the earlier emotional violence. The expressed intention is to prevent the reader from stopping halfway, to maintain a compelling momentum in the narrative, and this momentum also serves the vision of historical determinism by subjecting individuals to a sequence of violent events that is beyond their power to control.

What exactly Dickens means by beating his characters' own interest out of them is open to question. It might be taken to refer to the way in which they are forcibly harnessed to allegorical meanings, like Darnay with the "Everyman" implications of his original family name, or the sentimental equation of Lucie Manette with a "golden thread." But the only character who has any real interest to be beaten out of him, Carton, is not the object of any direct allegorizing. Indeed, in his case meaning is deliberately withheld rather than allegorically asserted, and no cogent reasons are offered for his alienation. This mystification has the effect of directing the search for significance away from the personal life towards the general condition of existence. Lukács's contention that Carton's fate is the one that least of all "grows organically out of the age and its social events" is justified only if the wider historical process is ignored, for it is as a victim of general social values and forces—and hence, by implication, of the historical continuum— that interest and significance are beaten out of him. As Lukács sees, he is a marginal figure, but he can be said to be significant precisely for that reason: he has been marginalized, so to speak, by the energy and values embodied in Stryver who, more properly than Darnay, is his *alter ego*. In his gloomy estrangement Carton suggests the neurotic price that may be exacted by the aggressive pursuit of individual success, by the bourgeois ethos of individual endeavor in its most crassly careerist form. The accusation that he levels at Stryver evinces a social as much as a personal truth: " 'You were always driving and riving and shouldering and pressing, to that restless degree that I had no chance for my life but in rust and repose.' " A world dominated by the energy and purpose of such as Stryver claims its moral and psychological victims within the dominant class. The triumph of the bourgeois will creates its opposite in the aimless, drifting existence of a character whose self-image—" 'I should ask . . . that I might be regarded as an useless . . . piece of furniture' "—betrays the marks of a reified consciousness. And to the extent that Stryver partakes of the violent spirit which is at work in the larger historical events, Carton comes to stand, too, as the victim of the catastrophic continuum of history, a role which he then, at the end, consciously assumes.

To define Carton in these terms is to spell out bluntly what is only intimated indirectly, for it is Dickens's refusal to define and explain precisely that gives Carton a greater degree of density and interest than the other characters. With Carton, indeed, Dickens comes closest to creating something like the mystery and opacity of individuality that he refers to in the "Night Shadows" meditation, but only up to a point, since in the final scenes of the character's transformation there is a movement back toward conventional coherence and transparency. If, as Benjamin argues, the meaning of the life of a character in a novel is revealed in his death, then Carton could be said to constitute himself as a character by choosing to die by the guillotine. He gives himself a goal and a purpose, and in so doing gives shape and meaning to his life. What has been aimless and indefinite becomes purposive and defined, and continuity is established between beginning and end, between promising youth and exemplary death. He achieves character in both a formal and a moral sense, and in the process realigns himself with the other representatives of English bourgeois life, exhibiting reflexes reminiscent of Stryver's in sensing a desire to strike the life out of the wood-sawyer and reflecting on the desirability of raising Madame Defarge's arm and striking under it sharp and deep.

Carton's transformation is clearly intended to be read as the redemption of a wasted life, but such a reading has to ignore the qualifying ambiguities that are involved in it. As he decides on his course of action, resolution is strangely mixed with fatalism:

> "There is nothing more to do," said he, glancing upward at the moon, "until tomorrow. I can't sleep."
>
> It was not a reckless manner, the manner in which he said these words aloud under the fast-sailing clouds, nor was it more expressive of negligence than defiance. It was the settled manner of a tired man, who had wandered and struggled and got lost, but who at length struck into his road and saw its end.

The term "end" carries a double meaning: in one sense it has to be read as "goal," stressing Carton's new-found sense of purpose and smuggling into the novel on the level of the individual life the positive teleology that is so markedly absent on the level of history. But the stronger meaning here is that of "conclusion," and a conclusion that is approached with a sense of release rather than a sense of achievement. The "tired man" is simply seeking repose, and in his desire for an end he makes explicit that resistance to the narrative and historical continuum which has been intimated elsewhere in the novel and now surfaces as the deepest yearning of a particular character.

He wishes to escape but, significantly, the mode of escape he chooses merely confirms his status as a victim of socio-historical circumstances. The act of self-sacrifice—an idea which haunts Dickens's imagination in this novel as powerfully and melodramatically as images of revolutionary violence—cannot be seen as simply the ultimate expression of altruism, since it is obscurely rooted in the same values that have significantly contributed to Carton's estrangement in the first place. The puritan ethic of disciplined personal endeavor demands renunciation such as Carton has been neurotically making all along, and its final act is the renunciation of life itself. Thus the very step which makes sense of his life is as perverse as it is noble, as much a capitulation to the uncontrollable forces that have governed his life as a transcendence of them. To seek to escape sacrifice by sacrificing oneself is the expression of a truly desperate desire for an ending.

These more questionable implications of Carton's self-chosen end are largely disguised by Dickens's narrative and rhetorical strategies in the closing chapters. The polarization and pathos of melodrama are engaged to elicit acceptance of him as an exemplary altruist, while the Christian rhetoric of death and resurrection serves to present his self-sacrifice as a positive act of redemption rather than an expression of world-weary resignation. The character is, as it were, borne along by an affective and rhetorical current which obscures contradictions, and this same current is clearly intended to carry the reader, unquestioning, from Carton's death under the Terror to the resurrection of civilized order in his prophetic vision of the future. This attempt to make the historical regeneration of France and the domestic happiness of the Darnays seem continuous with what has preceded them is, however, hardly convincing, as the only element of continuity is the continuing strain of imaginative resistance to the destructive historical continuum. That the historical process of escalating violence should issue in a benign future is scarcely conceivable in this context, and Dickens passes perfunctorily over how it could come about with a casual reference to "evil . . . gradually making expiation for itself and wearing out." The suggestion of entropy in that last phrase is significant. It is not so much a vision of redeeming historical development that is bestowed on Carton as a vision of the end of time. " 'There is no Time there,' " he says to the seamstress of the "better" land to which both are going; and his own vision of a better land, with its "beautiful city" and "brilliant people" rising from the abyss, appears similarly otherworldly, having a greater affinity with the New Jerusalem of the Apocalypse than with nineteenth-century Paris. Indeed, the apocalyptic note in this conclusion stresses finality rather than resurrection, and death haunts even the conventional pieties of the domestic happy ending: Lorry is seen "passing tranquilly to his reward" and the

Darnays, "their course done, lying side by side in their last earthly bed." Lives are shown passing to a peaceful end, and all this individual and historical "wearing out" is envisaged by a man who is himself gratefully embracing death as a welcome release. Even in his famous mawkish last words it is not the heroic deed but the long-sought repose, the "far, far better rest," that receives the final emphasis.

Weariness, both of character and of creative imagination, is the keynote of this ending, and it betrays the intellectual and imaginative impasse in which Dickens finds himself. Since he sees revolution as just another link in the chain of violence and oppression, and presents the efforts of individuals, like Darnay's journey to Paris, as powerless to influence the course of historical events, he can conceive no possibility, to use Benjamin's phrase, of blasting open the continuum of history by social and political action. Unlike Benjamin, Dickens can advance no alternative vision of time and history. The claim once made for *Middlemarch* [by J. Hillis Miller] that it replaces "the concepts of origin, end and continuity" by "the categories of repetition, of difference, of discontinuity, of openness" can certainly not be applied to *A Tale of Two Cities*. Origin and end, feudal oppression and revolutionary retribution, are linked by a causal chain which affirms the predominance of continuity. Repetition, on the other hand, as Dr. Manette's recurrent trauma illustrates, is here simply the mark of a mind imprisoned in the past, not a new, liberating category of temporal experience. Even the moments of discontinuity discussed earlier only challenge the narrative and historical continuum by revealing a desire to evade it. Carton's prophecy is simply a final evasive move, and one that gives itself away by its weary insistence on death and its eschatological suggestion of the end of time. Only by turning away from the course of human history can Dickens find a refuge for hope, and to express hope in such terms is tantamount to a confession of despair. In this novel of imprisonments and burials alive the writer himself remains imprisoned in a rigorously linear, end-determined narrative and the grimly determinist vision of history which it articulates. The resistance he offers is that of a mind vainly struggling to escape and thereby confirming the power of that which holds it captive. This vision of history as a catastrophic continuum is only made more powerful by the clear indications in the text that Dickens is expressing what is deeply repugnant to, yet stronger than, all that he can hope and wish for.

Chronology

1812 Charles John Huffam Dickens, the second of eight children, born February 7 to John and Elizabeth Dickens.

1814 John Dickens, a clerk in the Navy Pay Office, is transferred from Portsea to London. During these early years, from 1814 to 1821, Dickens is taught his letters by his mother, and he immerses himself in the fiction classics of his father's library.

1817 John Dickens moves family to Chatham.

1821 Dickens begins school with the son of a Baptist minister; he remains at this school for a time even after his family is transferred again to London in 1822.

1824 John Dickens is arrested for debt and sent to Marshalsea Prison, accompanied by his wife and younger children. Charles soon finds lodging in a poor neighborhood and begins work at Warren's Blacking Factory. His father is released three months later and Charles returns to school.

1824–26 Dickens attends Wellington House Academy, London.

1827 Works as a law clerk and spends time reading in the British Museum.

1830 Meets Maria Beadnell; he eventually falls in love with her, but she jilts him upon return from a trip to Paris in 1833.

1831 Becomes a reporter for the *Mirror of Parliament*.

1832 Becomes a staff writer for the *True Sun*.

1833 Dickens's first published piece, "A Dinner at Poplar Walk," appears in December issue of the *Monthly Magazine* under the pen name "Boz."

1834 Dickens becomes a staff writer on the *Morning Chronicle*. His "street sketches" begin to appear in the *Evening*

Chronicle. Dickens meets his future wife, Catherine Hogarth. Also, John Dickens is arrested again for debt.

1836   *Sketches by Boz,* illustrated by George Cruikshank, published. Dickens marries Catherine Hogarth in April. Also in this year, his first play, *The Strange Gentleman,* runs for two months at the St. James's Theatre. A second play, *The Village Coquettes,* is produced at the same theater. Dickens meets John Forster, who becomes a lifelong friend and his biographer.

1836–37   *Pickwick Papers* published in monthly installments from April through the following November.

1837   *Pickwick Papers* appears in book form. *Oliver Twist* begins to appear in *Bentley's Miscellany. Is She His Wife?* produced at the St. James's. Dickens's first child, a son, born, and the family moves to Doughty Street. Catherine's sister Mary, deeply loved by Dickens, dies suddenly.

1838   *Nicholas Nickleby* appears in installments; completed in October of 1839. Dickens's first daughter born.

1839   The Dickenses move to Devonshire Terrace. A second daughter born. *Nickleby* appears in book form.

1840   Dickens edits *Master Humphrey's Clock,* a weekly periodical, in which *The Old Curiosity Shop* appears.

1841   *Barnaby Rudge* appears in *Master Humphrey's Clock.* Another son born.

1842   Dickens and his wife tour America from January to June; Dickens publishes *American Notes* and begins *Martin Chuzzlewit.*

1843   *Martin Chuzzlewit* appears in monthly installments (January 1843–July 1844). *A Christmas Carol* published.

1844   Dickens tours Italy and Switzerland. Another Christmas book, *The Chimes,* completed. A third son born.

1845   Dickens produces *Every Man in his Humour* in England. *The Cricket on the Hearth* is written by Christmas, and Dickens begins *Pictures from Italy.* A fourth son born.

1846   Dickens creates and edits the *Daily News,* but resigns as editor after seventeen days. Begins *Dombey and Son* while in Lausanne; the novel appears in twenty monthly installments (October 1846–April 1848). *The Battle of Life: A Love Story* appears for Christmas.

1847   Dickens begins to manage a theatrical company and

arranges a benefit tour of *Every Man in his Humour*. Fifth son born.

1848   Daughter Fanny dies. Dickens's theatrical company performs for Queen Victoria. It also performs *The Merry Wives of Windsor* to raise money for the preservation of Shakespeare's birthplace. Dickens's last Christmas book, *The Haunted Man,* published.

1849   Dickens begins *David Copperfield* (published May 1849– November 1850). A sixth son born.

1850   *Household Words,* a weekly periodical, established with Dickens as editor. A third daughter born, who dies within a year.

1851   Dickens and his company participate in theatrical fund-raising. Dickens's father dies.

1852   *Bleak House* appears in monthly installments (March 1852– September 1853). The first bound volume of *A Child's History of England* appears. Dickens's last child, his seventh son, born.

1853   Dickens gives first public readings, from the Christmas books. Travels to France and Italy.

1854   *Hard Times* published in *Household Words* (April 1–August 12) and appears in book form.

1855   *Little Dorrit* appears in monthly installments (December 1855–June 1857). Dickens and family travel at year's end to Paris, where the novelist meets other leading literary and theatrical persons.

1856   Dickens purchases Gad's Hill Place, and the family returns to London.

1857   Dickens is involved primarily with theatrical productions.

1858   Dickens announces his separation from his wife, about which he writes a personal statement in *Household Words.*

1859   Dickens concludes *Household Words* and establishes a new weekly, *All the Year Round. A Tale of Two Cities* appears there from April 20 to November 26, and is published in book form in December.

1860   *Great Expectations* underway in weekly installments (December 1860–August 1861).

1861   *The Uncommercial Traveller,* a collection of pieces from *All the Year Round,* published.

1862   Dickens gives many public readings and travels to Paris.

1863 Dickens continues his readings in Paris and London. Daughter Elizabeth dies.

1864 *Our Mutual Friend* appears in monthly installments for publisher Chapman and Hall (May 1864–November 1865).

1865 Dickens suffers a stroke that leaves him lame. Involved in train accident, which causes him to change the ending of *Our Mutual Friend*. *Our Mutual Friend* appears in book form. The second collection of *The Uncommercial Traveller* published.

1866 Dickens gives thirty public readings in the English provinces.

1867 Continues the provincial readings, then travels to America in November, where he reads in Boston and New York. This tour permanently breaks the novelist's health.

1868 In April, Dickens returns to England, where he continues to tour.

1869 The first public reading of the murder of Nancy (from *Oliver Twist*) performed, but his doctors recommend he discontinue the tour. *The Mystery of Edwin Drood* begun.

1870 Dickens gives twelve readings in London. Six parts of *Edwin Drood* appear from April to September. On June 9, Charles Dickens dies, aged 58. He is buried in the Poets' Corner, Westminster Abbey.

Contributors

HAROLD BLOOM, Sterling Professor of the Humanities at Yale University, is the author of *The Anxiety of Influence, Poetry and Repression,* and many other volumes of literary criticism. His forthcoming study, *Freud: Transference and Authority,* attempts a full-scale reading of all of Freud's major writings. A MacArthur Prize Fellow, he is general editor of five series of literary criticism published by Chelsea House. During 1987–88, he was appointed Charles Eliot Norton Professor of Poetry at Harvard University.

ROBERT ALTER is Professor of Hebrew and Comparative Literature at the University of California, Berkeley. His books include *Defenses of the Imagination* and *Partial Magic: The Novel as a Self-Conscious Genre.*

DAVID D. MARCUS teaches at the University of Illinois at Chicago Circle.

ALBERT D. HUTTER is Associate Professor of English and Comparative Literature at the University of California, Los Angeles, and a research psychoanalyst at the Southern California Psychoanalytic Institute.

JOHN KUCICH is Associate Professor of English at the University of Michigan, Ann Arbor. He is the author of *Excess and Restraint in the Novels of Charles Dickens.*

CATHERINE GALLAGHER is Assistant Professor of English at the University of Delaware.

EDWIN M. EIGNER, Professor of English and Creative Writing at the University of California, Riverside, is the author of *The Metaphysical Novel in England and America: Dickens, Bulwer, Hawthorne, Melville.*

GARRETT STEWART is Profesor of English at the University of

California, Santa Barbara. He is the author of *Dickens and the Trials of Imagination* and *Death Sentences: Styles of Dying in British Fiction*.

J. M. RIGNALL is Lecturer in English and Comparative Literature at the University of Warwick.

Bibliography

Baumgarten, Murray. "Writing the Revolution." *Dickens Studies Annual* 12 (1983): 161–76.

Beckwith, Charles E., ed. *Twentieth-Century Interpretations of* A Tale of Two Cities: *A Collection of Critical Essays.* Englewood Cliffs, N.J.: Prentice-Hall, 1972.

Collins, Philip, ed. *Dickens: The Critical Heritage.* London: Routledge & Kegan Paul, 1971.

Court, Franklin E. "Boots, Barbarism, and the New Order in Dickens's *Tale of Two Cities.*" *Victorians Institute Journal* 9 (1980–81): 29–37.

Dunn, Richard J. "A Tale of Two Dramatists." *Dickens Studies Annual* 12 (1983): 117–24.

Dyson, A.E. *The Inimitable Dickens: A Reading of the Novels.* London: Macmillan, 1970.

Eigner, Edwin M. *The Metaphysical Novel in England and America: Dickens, Bulwer, Hawthorne, Melville.* Berkeley: University of California Press, 1978.

Ford, George H. *Dickens and His Readers: Aspects of Novel Criticism since 1836.* Princeton: Princeton University Press, 1955.

Ford, George H., and Lauriat Lane, Jr., eds. *The Dickens Critics.* Ithaca: Cornell University Press, 1961.

Forster, John. *The Life of Charles Dickens,* edited by A. J. Hoppé. 2 vols. London: Dent, 1966.

Frank, Lawrence. *Charles Dickens and the Romantic Self.* Lincoln: University of Nebraska Press, 1984.

Gilbert, Elliot L. " 'To Awake from History': Carlyle, Thackery, and *A Tale of Two Cities.*" *Dickens Studies Annual* 12 (1983): 247–65.

Gold, Joseph. *Charles Dickens: Radical Moralist.* Minneapolis: University of Minnesota Press, 1972.

Gross, John. *"A Tale of Two Cities."* In *Dickens and The Twentieth Century,* edited by John Gross and Gabriel Pearson, 187–98. London: Routledge & Kegan Paul, 1962.

Haig, Stirling. "Frenglish in *A Tale of Two Cities.*" *Dickens Studies Annual* 11 (1983): 93–97.

Hollington, Michael. *Dickens and the Grotesque.* Totowa, N.J.: Barnes & Noble, 1984.

Hutter, Albert D. "The Novelist as Resurrectionist: Dickens and the Dilemma of Death." *Dickens Studies Annual* 12 (1983): 1–33.

Jackson, T. A. *Charles Dickens: The Progress of a Radical.* New York: International Publishers, 1938.

Johnson, Edgar H. *Charles Dickens: His Tragedy and Triumph.* Rev. ed. London: Allen Lane, 1977.

Kucich, John. *Excess and Restraint in the Novels of Charles Dickens.* Athens: University of Georgia Press, 1981.

Lindley, Dwight N. "Clio and Three Historical Novels." *Dickens Studies Annual* 10 (1982): 77–99.

Lindsay, Jack. *"A Tale of Two Cities." Life and Letters and The London Mercury* 62 (1949): 191–204.

Lukács, Georg. *The Historical Novel,* translated by Hannah and Stanley Mitchell. Harmondsworth: Penguin, 1969.

MacKay, Carol Hanbery. "The Rhetoric of Soliloquy in *The French Revolution* and *A Tale of Two Cities.*" *Dickens Studies Annual* 12 (1983): 197–207.

Manheim, Leonard. "A Tale of Two Characters: A Study in Multiple Projection." *Dickens Studies Annual* 1 (1970): 225–37.

Mengle, Ewald. "The Poisoned Fountain: Dickens' Use of a Traditional Symbol." *The Dickensian* 80 (Spring 1984): 26–32.

Miller, J. Hillis. *Charles Dickens: The World of His Novels.* Cambridge: Harvard University Press, 1958.

Monod, Sylvère. "Some Stylistic Devices in *A Tale of Two Cities.*" In *Dickens the Craftsman: Strategies of Presentation,* edited by Robert B. Partlow, Jr., 165–86. Carbondale: Southern Illinois University Press, 1970.

———. "Dickens' Attitudes in *A Tale of Two Cities.*" In *Dickens Centennial Essays,* edited by Ada Nisbet and Blake Nevius. London: University of California Press, 1971.

Nelson, Harland S. *Charles Dickens.* Boston: Twayne, 1981.

Oddie, William. *Dickens and Carlyle: The Question of Influence.* London: Centenary, 1972.

Pratt, Branwen Bailey. "Carlyle and Dickens: Heroes and Hero-Worshipers." *Dickens Studies Annual* 12 (1983): 223–46.

Sanders, Andrew. "Monsieur heretofore the Marquis: Dickens' St. Evrémonde." *The Dickensian* 77 (Autumn 1981): 148–56.

Spence, Gordon. "Dickens as a Historical Novelist." *The Dickensian* 72 (1976): 21–30.

Sterrenburg, Lee. "Psychoanalysis and the Iconography of Revolution." *Victorian Studies* 19 (1975): 241–64.

Stoehr, Taylor. *Dickens: The Dreamer's Stance.* Ithaca: Cornell University Press, 1965.

Thurley, Geoffrey. *The Dickens Myth: Its Genesis and Structure.* London: Routledge & Kegan Paul, 1976.

Timko, Michael. "Splendid Impressions and Picturesque Means: Dickens, Carlyle, and the French Revolution." *Dickens Studies Annual* 12 (1983): 177–95.

Acknowledgments

"The Demons of History in Dicken's *Tale*" by Robert Alter from *Motives for Fiction* by Robert Alter, © 1984 by Robert Alter. Reprinted by permission of Harvard University Press. This essay originally appeared in *Novel: A Forum on Fiction* 2, no. 2 (Winter 1969), © 1969 by Novel Corp. Reprinted by permission.

"The Carlylean Vision of *A Tale of Two Cities*" by David D. Marcus from *Studies in the Novel* 8, no. 1 (Spring 1976), © 1976 by North Texas State University. Reprinted by permission.

"Nation and Generation in *A Tale of Two Cities*" by Albert D. Hutter from *PMLA* 93, no.3 (May 1978), © 1978 by the Modern Language Association of America. Reprinted by permission of the Modern Language Association of America.

"The Purity of Violence: *A Tale of Two Cities*" by John Kucich from *Dickens Studies Annual* 8 (1980), © 1980 by AMS Press, Inc. Reprinted by permission of AMS Press, Inc.

"The Duplicity of Doubling in *A Tale of Two Cities*" by Catherine Gallagher from *Dickens Studies Annual* 12 (1983), © 1983 by AMS Press, Inc. Reprinted by permission of AMS Press, Inc.

"Charles Darnay and Revolutionary Identity" by Edwin M. Eigner from *Dickens Studies Annual* 12 (1983), © 1983 by AMS Press, Inc. Reprinted by permission of AMS Press, Inc.

"Death by Water in *A Tale of Two Cities*" (originally entitled "Chapter 2") by Garrett Stewart from *Death Sentences: Styles of Dying in British Fiction* by Garrett Stewart, © 1984 by the President and Fellows of Harvard University. Reprinted by permission of Harvard University Press.

"Dickens and the Catastrophic Continuum of History in *A Tale of Two Cities*" by J. M. Rignall from *ELH* 51, no. 3 (Fall 1984), © 1984 by the Johns Hopkins University Press, Baltimore/London. Reprinted by permission of the Johns Hopkins University Press.

Index